To Vince
Very Best Wishes
Greg + Max xx

CHRIS JEFFCOATE & JACKIE KUFLIK

In memory of Kirsten Embleton-Black,
a lecturer at Brooklands College,
who died a victim of Breast Cancer at the age of 34.

ACKNOWLEDGEMENTS

As with all ventures where a lot of people are involved there are many to be thanked. This venture is no exception. This acknowledgement is no exception to the rule that some will not be mentioned, not because we have forgotten what they have done or when, or how, but because we have run out of space.

Thank You

Silver Spoon - for sponsorship
Cake Art - for distribution
Brooklands College - for sponsorship
Chez - at the very least for taking the worry away
Terri - for supporting us behind the scenes
Our classes - for battling on regardless
Our colleagues - for the cover
Gill - for relentlessly chasing us with phone messages
Team at BREAKTHROUGH - for your belief, support and encouragement (when we thought our job was supporting you)
Eileen Swann - for pushing us in the first place
British Sugarcraft Guild - for your goodwill in so many ways
Paul Toner - for your artistic vision
Linda and Mike O'Neill - for being first to say 'yes' - the shots are brilliant
Steve Pullinger - for special equipment
To all our fundraisers - for doing it
To our families, Brian, Michelle, Alistair and Richard Jeffcoate and Sam and Jo Kuflik, who continually believed that their mothers were somewhere (but not sure where) but still love us regardless.

Published in 1993 by Jeffcoate & Kuflik, 6 Aspen Gardens, Hook, Hampshire, RG27 9RB

ISBN 0 9521532 0 3

Edited by Chris Jeffcoate and Jackie Kuflik
Designed by Paul Toner, Artwork by Paul Stratford
Insight Communications, Ascot, Berkshire
Creative Photography by Mike O'Neill Associates, Slough, Berkshire
Portrait Photography by Alison Trapmore, Oatlands Studio, Weybridge,Surrey
Printed by Hawthornes, New Basford, Nottingham
Colour Seperations by Manor Graphics, Ilkeston, Derbyshire
Distributed by Cake Art Limited, Taunton, Somerset

CONTENTS

Foreword

INTRODUCTION

Does the learning ever stop? Interactive teaching produces work where both student and tutor gain knowledge from a venture into the creative world. What perhaps makes this book and its contents very special is that it has been filled with the variety and ingenuity of many people, giving of their time and effort whilst taking pleasure in their artform, for the benefit of BREAKTHROUGH Breast Cancer.

We are delighted to have achieved our objective;

"to create a collection of new designs and innovative ideas to inspire the students of the future, the experts of today and to communicate the joys and pleasures of working in this creative medium to like minded people."

Chris Jeffcoate and Jackie Kuflik

May 1993

Chris Jeffcoate LCGI

Chris' first steps in sugarwork were taken in her grandmothers bakery from where her knowledge in bread, confectionery and sugarwork has developed. As a lecturer at Brooklands College, Chris has shared her knowledge in many ways as well as her work for City and Guilds of London Institute as Chief Regional Assessor for 121 Design and Decoration of Flour Confectionery, as technical Consultant of 7900 Creative Studies, Sugarcraft, both Parts One and Two, and is an External Verifier. She is a member of the British Sugarcraft Guild, Chairman of their Development and Training Committee, a Judge and Demonstrator.

Jackie Kuflik

Jackie is a lecturer at Brooklands College to which she has brought a variety of talents from a career path which has included the travel industry and marketing as well as her own business in celebration cakes. She is now an External Verifier for City and Guilds and a member and Demonstrator of the British Sugarcraft Guild.

BREAKTHROUGH Breast Cancer was set up to raise £15,000,000 to create a Breast Cancer Research Centre dedicated to eradicating the disease.

Other concerns have been cured. BREAKTHROUGH believes it is time Breast Cancer was added to the list.

Registered Charity no.328323

P.O.Box 2JP, London W1A 2JP

It has been a pleasure working with Jackie Kuflik and Chris Jeffcoate and their students on this superb book of sugarcraft skill and innovation.

It is their dedication and commitment to combating this terrible disease that has been the true inspiration for this book and for this we are forever grateful.

Gill Theodoresen

Director

BREAKTHROUGH Breast Cancer

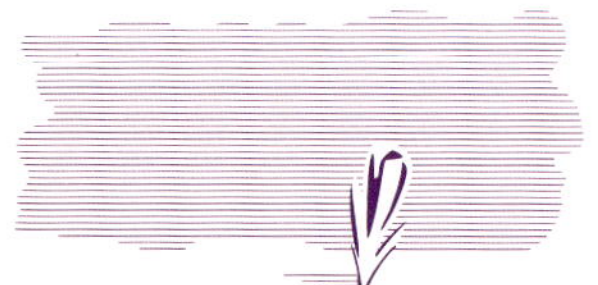

BREAKTHROUGH

BREAST CANCER

Foreword

It is a great pleasure for me to be associated with this fine project to support such a worthwhile cause as BREAKTHROUGH Breast Cancer. I first saw the work of the Brooklands Sugarcraft Team when I visited the college in 1991 and was impressed then with the highly charged creative atmosphere in which the students worked. I hope that you will feel some of this atmosphere through the pages of this book and that you will be inspired to create some of the work enclosed.

All our lives are touched in some way by breast cancer, through the suffering of friends and family, and I thank you for your contribution in buying and enjoying this publication.

Cliff Richard

As one of the pioneers in Sugarcraft and a founder member and Past President of the British Sugarcraft Guild it gives me the greatest pleasure in supporting Chris and Jackie, their colleagues and students in this wonderful venture. I have known Chris (and through her, Jackie) for many years and greatly admire their expertise, not only for the full range of beautifully executed sugar works but also for their knowledge, excellent teaching and organising ability.

Chris and I worked very closely together in the development of the 7900 Sugarcraft Course in Creative Studies, a new course involving sugarcraft in its art form which not only develops the students character and personality but will enrich their lives forever.

I respect the Brooklands Sugarcraft Team for their training of sugarcraft teachers throughout the country and for the high standard and original work produced.

I give my wholehearted support to this project, Sweet Charity, and the way in which it contributes to BREAKTHROUGH Breast Cancer, a cause dear to my heart, being a victim myself.

I appeal to everyone reading this to think deeply and contribute in any way you can.

With my continued love and support, to you both, Chris and Jackie,
Eileen Swann

I am very pleased to support this project and delighted that people have all worked together to produce such an interesting book and so benefit such a worthwhile charity, BREAKTHROUGH Breast Cancer, in this way. The friendships made and sharing of our craft is of great benefit to all those who take part, whether at colleges or through the British Sugarcraft Guild.

Janet McCreedy
National Secretary
British Sugarcraft Guild

Avocado Bavarois with Lychee, Strawberry and Avocado Coulis

AVOCADO BAVAROIS

with Lychee, Strawberry and Avocado Coulis

This plated sweet stems from an article I wrote in Chef Magazine when I discussed how the skills of the sugarcraft expert could easily by transferred to the work of the patissier. The sweet uses ingredients and techniques as well as skills familiar to the sugarcraft practitioner.

Ingredients (for four servings)

2 Avocados
1 punnet Strawberries
Juice of 3/4 lemon
50g (2oz) Silver Spoon caster sugar
6 leaves gelatine (or 1 sachet powdered)
1 Strawberry Jelly (or 25g Jelly crystals)
8 Lychees
50g (2oz) Silver Spoon icing sugar
1 tub Fromage Frais (125ml)
125ml White Wine

Preparing the mould

Melt the strawberry jelly and pour into 4 heart moulds, which have been placed on silicon paper on a tray, to 0.5cm thickness. Allow to set in the fridge. 2.When set, cut four strawberries into a fan shape and place carefully on to the set jelly, using a little of the unset jelly. Return to the fridge to set. 3. When set, lightly oil the inside of the mould, NOT the jelly.

The Bavarois

1. Liquidise one avocado pear with four peeled lychees and the juice of half a lemon with 50g (2oz) of icing sugar, making sure the mixture is very smooth. Place in a mixing bowl. 2. Soak 4 leaves of leaf gelatine in cold water to soften them then heat in a pan until dissolved. (If powdered gelatine is used soak in a little water and then boil) Add this to the avocado and lychee puree, mix well and allow to cool in the fridge. 3. Chop up six ripe strawberries and add to the mixture. 4. As the mixture starts to set add half the fromage frais and mix in carefully. 5. Pour into the prepared moulds and set in the fridge.

Avocado Coulis

1. Puree one avocado with 50g (2oz) caster sugar, the wine and a few drops of lemon juice. (Note: it is essential that the coulis is kept chilled in an airtight container before being used or preferably made just prior to being eaten.

To decorate and serve

1. Turn the moulded Bavarois on to a plate with the jelly side uppermost and remove the paper. (If the jelly is a little dull due to the silicon paper, quickly flash the jelly under a hot grill for a very short time and replace back in the fridge to set for a couple of minutes). 2. Carefully run the point of a warm knife around the edge of the jelly and lift off the mould. 3. Pour some coulis to the side of the mould and drop a few spots of thin fromage frais on the top, then pull a cocktail stick through the spots to give a heart shape effect. 4. Decorate with a strawberry dusted in icing sugar and a lychee cut down the sides and folded back. 5. Finally finish by arranging the leaves.

Leaf mixture
100g (4oz) Silver Spoon icing sugar
1 egg white
Juice quarter lemon
100g (4oz) Ground hazelnuts
Zest 1 lemon

Sieve icing sugar and hazelnuts into a small bowl. Add grated zest of lemon, egg white and lemon juice and mix to a smooth paste. Prepare the template and spread the paste with a palette knife or scraper through the template on to small squares of silicon paper. (For ease of handling, each leaf should be on a separate piece of paper). Bake in a hot oven(Gas Mark 7/220° C/425° F) for approximately 3 to 4 minutes to a light brown colour. Remove from the oven and quickly press the leaves on to a metal leaf mould and twist each leaf into shape. (This must be done quickly otherwise the leaves will harden. Only cook 5 or 6 leaves at a time). When the leaves are cold, remove the silicon paper and store until required in a air tight container.

Adrian Clement has had wide industrial experience as a chef, waiter, restaurant and bars manager and is now a Senior Lecturer in Food Studies at Brooklands College.

Amy

AMY

Instructions

Cut the cake from a round fruit cake using diagram A as a guide. Marzipan and sugarpaste the cake and board. Mix together sugarpaste and flowerpaste (to give strength) for the pleated edge and the tablecloth. Make the pleats half the depth of the cake and attach to the cake.

For the tablecloth, roll the paste very thinly and use diagram B to cut the shape (approximately 2"/5cm larger than cake). Snip a small cut where shown as this will help ease the tablecloth into position. Make sure the tablecloth hangs over the top of the pleats.

Make the brush embroidered lace and leave to dry. Pipe the stems and some of the leaves from the embroidery pattern directly on to the edge of the cloth, attaching the lace as shown. Use the brush embroidery technique for the Magnolia pattern and the name is made as a runout motif and glued to the cake with a little royal icing when dry.

The butterfly

Brush embroider the wings on to wax paper and leave to dry. Dust with colour. Pipe the body with royal icing and carefully place the wings into the soft sugar, support if necessary and leave to dry.Make the Magnolia flowers and arrange as shown.

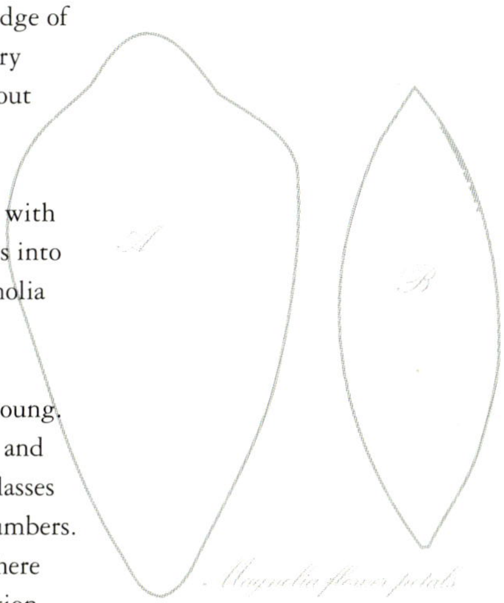

Cake decoration started for Paddi Clarke when the children were young. "I so enjoyed creating E.T.'s with lit finger, monkeys climbing and standing palm trees that I decided this must go further! Evening classes and courses and City and Guilds qualifications followed in their numbers. It kind of takes you over, doesn't it? Which brings me to today, where courses and qualifications and the odd demonstration and competition success still continue, but along the way I started to teach the subject which is stimulating, rewarding and fun."

Paddi has been working in sugar for at least 8 years, is currently studying Part II at Brooklands and continues to inspire all her students at the four Adult Education Centres where she teaches.

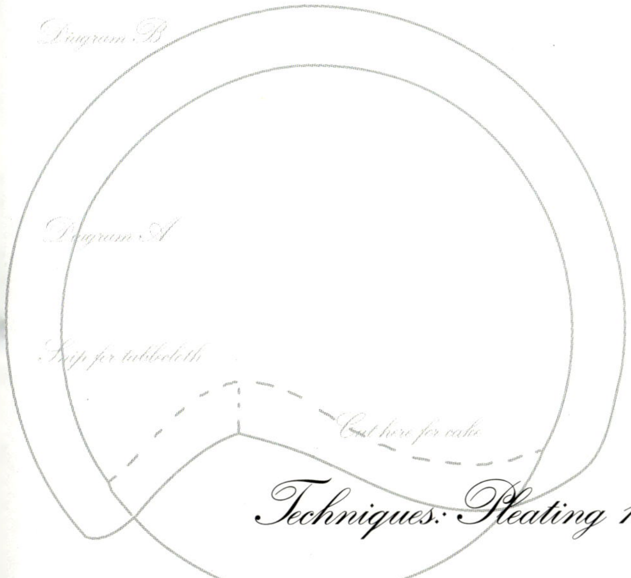

Techniques: Pleating 1, Runouts, Brush embroidery, Flowers

APRICOT & CHOCOLATE GATEAU

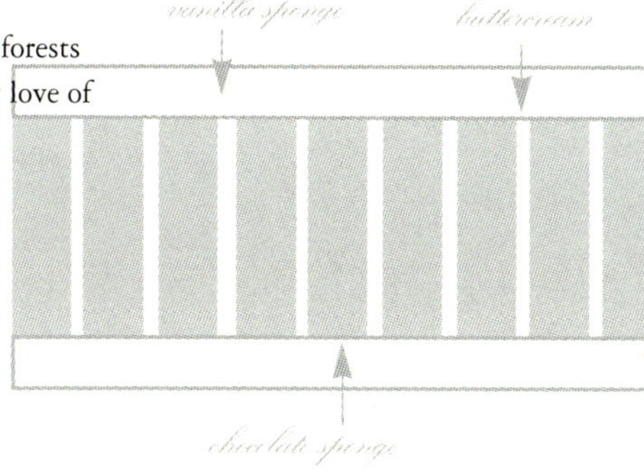

I am born in October. The autumn is one of the times when the forests glow in the most beautiful colours. I have tried to combine my love of nature and painting in the design of this gateau.

You will need:
1 sheet vanilla sponge (see swiss roll recipe)
1 sheet chocolate sponge
chocolate buttercream
apricots in brandy
light brown marzipan for covering
darker brown marzipan for the tree
1 oval marzipan plaque
plain buttercream
piping chocolate
oval cake board

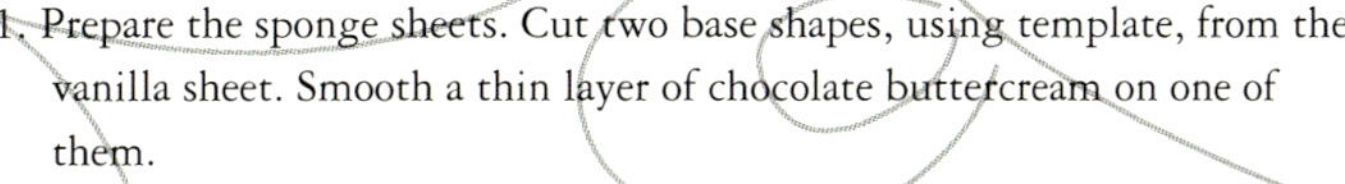

1. Prepare the sponge sheets. Cut two base shapes, using template, from the vanilla sheet. Smooth a thin layer of chocolate buttercream on one of them.
2. Cut the chocolate sheet into approximately 2cm strips and spread on a layer of chocolate buttercream. Chop up the apricots into small pieces and sprinkle over the buttercream. Roll up the strips to build one big snail and two smaller ones and assemble on to the vanilla base. Smooth the surface with a little chocolate buttercream and position the second vanilla base on top. Cover the whole with a thin layer of chocolate buttercream.
3. Roll out the light brown marzipan and cut a strip for the sides of the gateau, texture with a lined rolling pin. Apply this to the gateau and neatly trim the top edge. Cover the top with the remainder of the marzipan and then trim to size. (The join of marzipan will be on the sides of the cake and not the top). Chill the gateau.
4. Prepare the oval plaque from marzipan. Colour the plain buttercream with a variety of autumn colours, e.g. three shades of green, orange, red, brown, blue and purple (for the sky). Apply the buttercream with a paintbrush and chill the plaque before placing it into position on the gateau.
5. Model a half moon from white marzipan, roll long thin sausages of the dark brown marzipan to make the tree.
6. Decorate the gateau with piping chocolate (melted chocolate covering with a few drops of water added) and small yellow flowers made with plunger or ejector cutters.

Carmen Odgaard was born in Germany and came to Britain in 1987. After finishing a two year apprenticeship as a confectioner she looked for a new challenge and found it in City and Guilds 121 course. She was instantly hooked and has just completed the City and Guilds 7900 Creative Studies course - in a year! (Carmen has moved to Denmark as this book is being written - we wish her happiness and success CJ/JK)

base shape

Bamboo

BAMBOO

Instructions

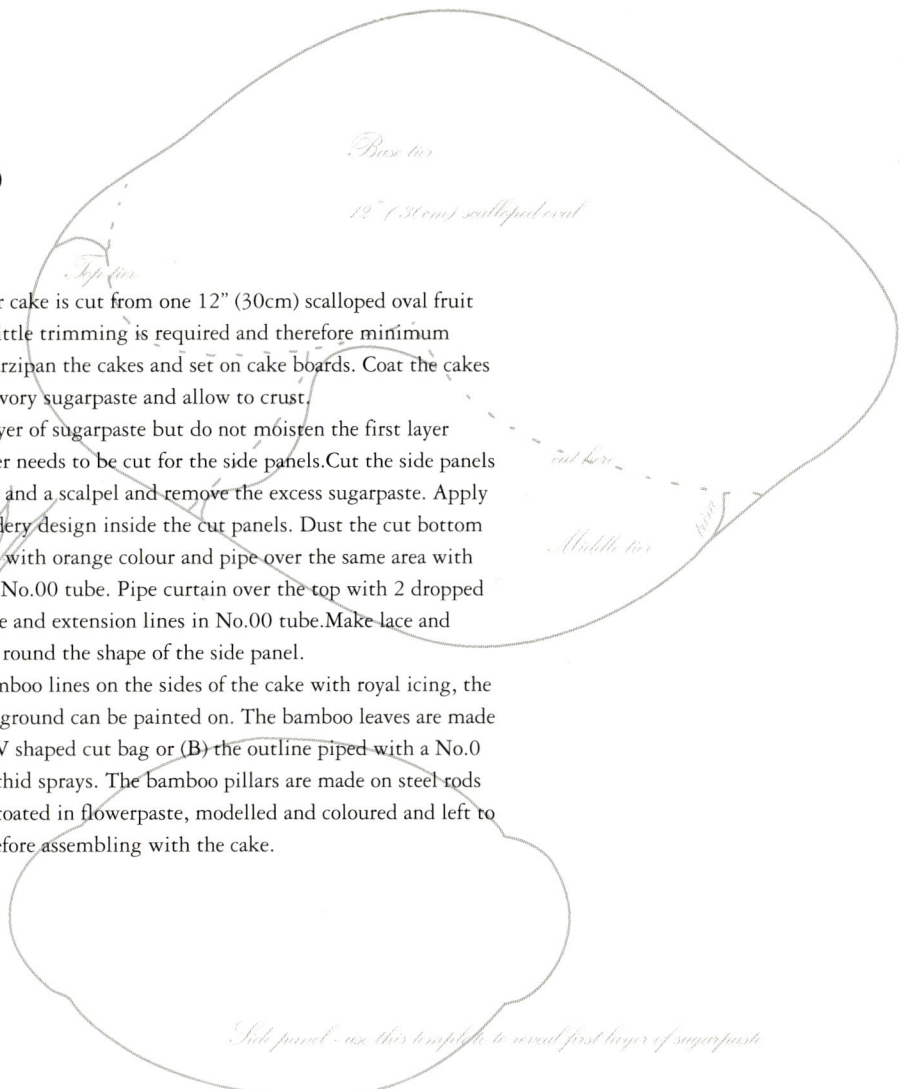

This three tier cake is cut from one 12" (30cm) scalloped oval fruit cake. Very little trimming is required and therefore minimum wastage. Marzipan the cakes and set on cake boards. Coat the cakes in a thin layer of ivory sugarpaste and allow to crust.

Apply a second layer of sugarpaste but do not moisten the first layer where the top layer needs to be cut for the side panels.Cut the side panels with the template and a scalpel and remove the excess sugarpaste. Apply the brush embroidery design inside the cut panels. Dust the cut bottom edge of the panels with orange colour and pipe over the same area with extension lines in No.00 tube. Pipe curtain over the top with 2 dropped loops in No.1 tube and extension lines in No.00 tube.Make lace and attach all the way round the shape of the side panel.

Pipe the main bamboo lines on the sides of the cake with royal icing, the others in the background can be painted on. The bamboo leaves are made either (A) with a V shaped cut bag or (B) the outline piped with a No.0 tube.Make the orchid sprays. The bamboo pillars are made on steel rods which have been coated in flowerpaste, modelled and coloured and left to dry thoroughly before assembling with the cake.

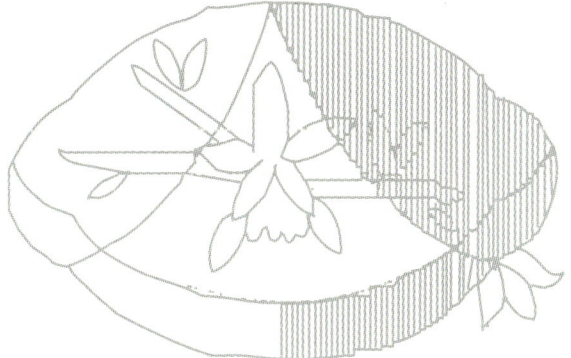

Paddi Clarke

Techniques: Extension work, Brush embroidery, Pressure piping, Lace, Flowers, Painting

Black and White

BLACK AND WHITE

Russian architecture was the inspiration for this wedding cake with a difference.

Instructions

Assemble the boards and cakes as shown in the diagram. The cakes and boards are coated in marzipan and sugarpaste. The ornamentation is made from pastillage and enhanced with piped royal icing.

Cards - cut from thinly rolled pastillage, dry over curved formers and use to decorate edge of bottom tier. Other cards are dried into irregular shapes and used to decorate top edge of middle tier. The centre panel of each card is painted with black food colouring - take great care with the edges.

Side panels - use template to cut these and leave to dry on a flat surface before applying them to the side of the middle tier.

Pillars - rib roll pastillage, cut to required size and dry over curved formers. Attach to corners of middle tier.

Textured design - used either commercial moulds, hand moulding or pressure piping and apply in archways on middle tier.

Pressure piped design - apply the pattern shown to the sides of the top tier.

Top piece - moulded in two halves and joined together. Cover the joins with piped cornelli work. You may need to hunt around for suitable objects to act as formers for this - we used a half banister knob and a cone shaped container, glued together. The pastillage was dried over the top of this.

Lorraine Dicker has a great enthusiasm for sugarcraft, originally gained from helping her mum with the cake decorating. At only 19 years old, Lorraine is a qualified baker, confectioner and cake decorator and is continuing studying at Brooklands for 7900 Creative Studies course. She is no stranger to excellence, having achieved Distinction grades in her qualifications and the Top Student for Cake Decorating Award at Brooklands for 1992/3.

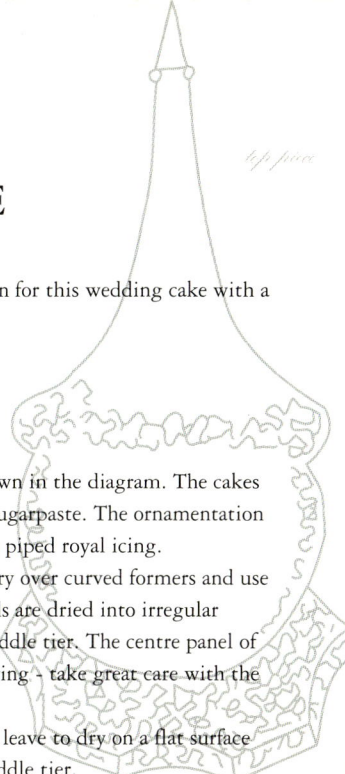

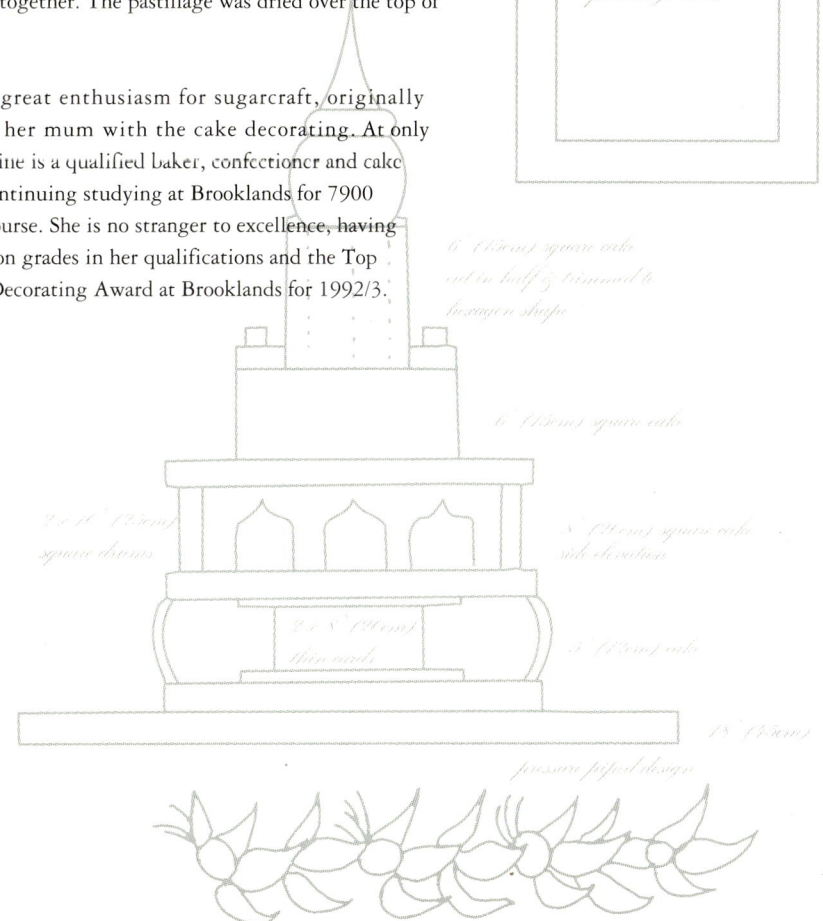

Techniques: Pastillage

Blackberry

BLACKBERRY

I wanted to create a wedding cake with a seasonal theme using strong, natural colours on a pure, white background. However, I also wanted to try making the cake look as if it was floating.

Instructions

Marzipan and coat in royal icing two cakes set on cake cards of the same size as the cakes. On the final coat use a scraper with two semi circular cut outs to leave two raised curved lines.To prepare the boards, take one round cake drum 3" (7.5cm) larger than the cake and another 1" (2.5cm) smaller for each tier. Glue these boards together and coat in royal icing, finishing with a chamfered edge made with a palette knife held at an angle. When dry, stick cakes in position with royal icing (keeping the thin card in place).

Embroider blackberry design on side of cakes between raised lines.Make paper templates as shown in diagrams and use these as patterns for linework and filigree.Pipe stringwork at bottom of each cake edge (see diagram).Make cake pillar by cutting out 3 discs from sheet polystyrene, 5"(12.5cm) 4.5"(11cm) and 3.5" (9cm) using a sharp knife and rounding off the edges. Coat each section in sugarpaste and glue together with royal icing.

Top ornament. Using pastillage cut out 3 of template A and 2 of template B and dry over a rolling pin to curve. Model a series of flat circles, decreasing in size and a top pointed dome shape. Glue petal shapes on to 2 bottom discs then glue all discs together with royal icing. Pipe dots on edges of petal shapes.Make blackberries, blossoms and leaves and arrange to complete the design.

Lorraine Dicker

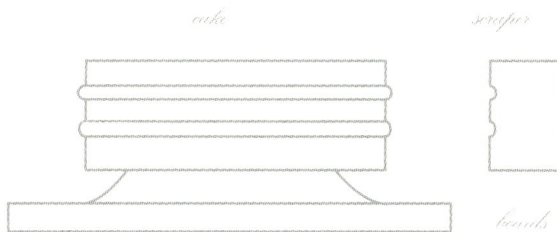

Techniques: Embroidery, Stringwork, Pastillage,

Butterfly

BUTTERFLY

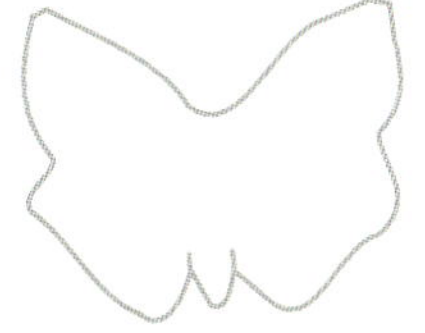

My favourite area of sugarcraft is making sugar flowers and this in part inspired me to make this cake. I wanted it to be different but was stuck for an idea until it was suggested to me that I could make 'fantasy' flowers with butterfly wings. I designed three 'butterfly flowers' which I have used here on a cake based on the shape of the Monarch Butterfly.

Instructions

The template for this cake is shown reduced by 50%. Therefore, enlarge the template and cut the shape from a slab of cake and coat the whole in a layer of marzipan. Build up areas 1 and 2 with sugarpaste to give greater definition of the butterfly wings. Smooth joins well and then coat the whole cake in a layer of sugarpaste.

Pipe a line of bulbs (No.1 tube) along the base of the cake and leave to dry. Petal dust the bottom half of the cake in pale green, brushing the colour on in upward strokes. Petal dust the cake in the dotted area on template. Transfer the side design on to the cake, stencil the leaves and then pipe the stems with No.1 tube. The flowers are two small shells piped together. Pipe the lines on to the top of the cake in pale green royal icing using a No.1 tube and overpiping in a darker green with a No.0 tube.

Make the 'butterfly flowers' and arrange on the cake.

Lynsey Fairbairn became interested in sugarcraft when she was 15 and is now completing Bakery and Sugarcraft courses at Brooklands. She has recently won medals at National competition level and has been awarded the Renshaw Cup as Top Student for 1992/3 at Brooklands College.

1.

2.

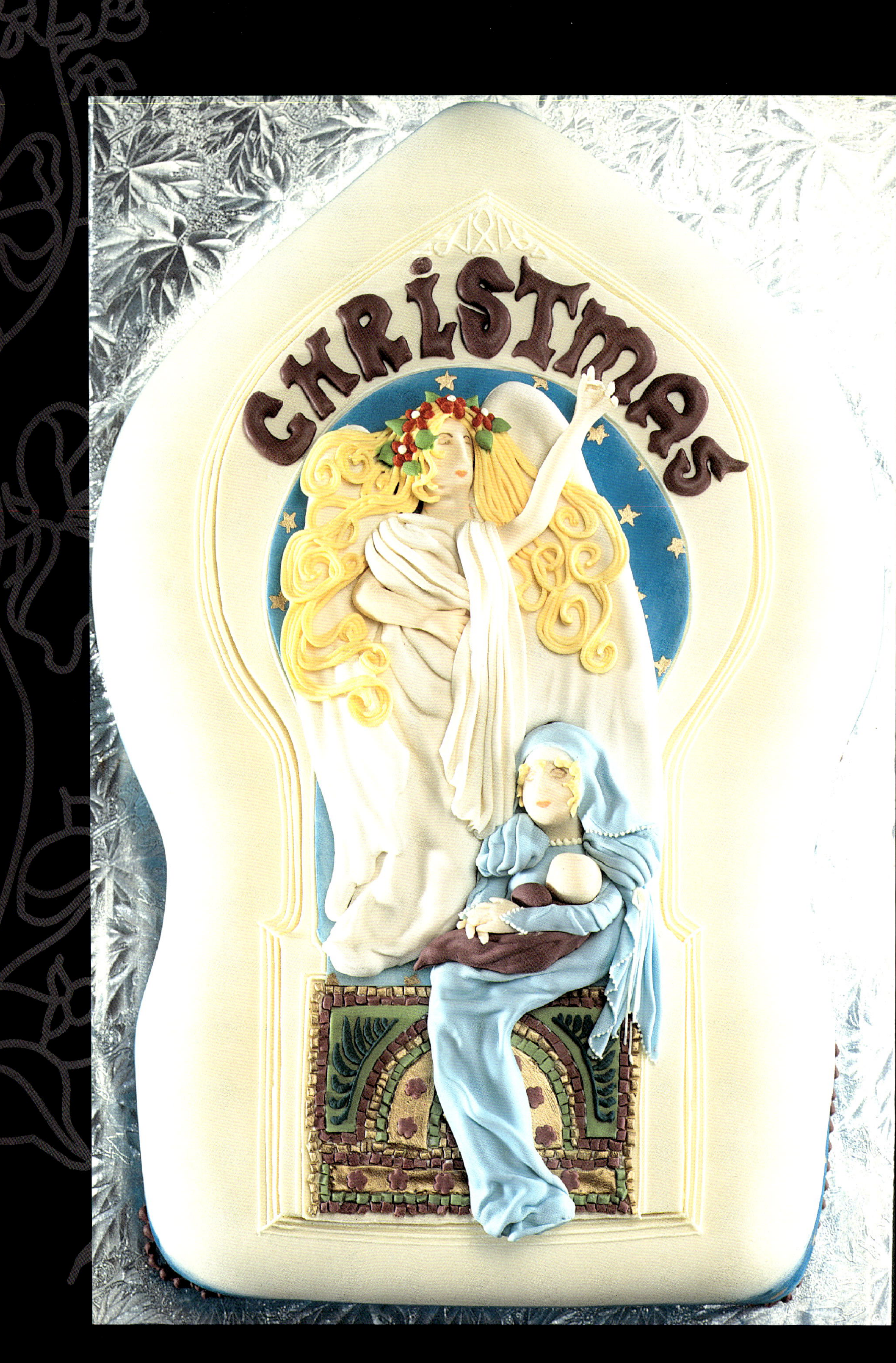

Christmas

CHRISTMAS

Madeliene Hodgetts is studying Bakery, Cake Decoration and Creative Studies at Brooklands College as a full time student. She plans to take a Business Studies course as she hopes in the future to have her own cake business. Madeliene is very interested in Art Nouveau and Art Deco, being particularly fascinated by their use of colour and stylised shapes. It was from that period that she was inspired to make this cake.

Instructions

Use template A to cut out the shape of the cake enlarging by A, B and C to cut out plaques from cream coloured sugarpaste. These three plaques should be left to dry completely.Make mosaic pattern on plaque C. Secure plaque B to plaque A and assemble all the plaques to the cake top. Make the figures and set in position, painting in features and piping hair with No.1 tube. Finish with 2,1,0 linework around plaques.

Dust dark blue around the sides of the cake and stencil gold stars over the blue. Pipe a row of bulbs in burgundy colour around the bottom edge of the cake.

Make the lettering in runouts and attach to the cake when dry.

Techniques: Relief 4, Runouts, Mosaic

Photo: John Rawling

Clematis

CLEMATIS

Alison Proctor made this cake for her son's wedding. The embroidery design was taken from the brides dress. The cake was kept very simple to show the flowers to their best effect.

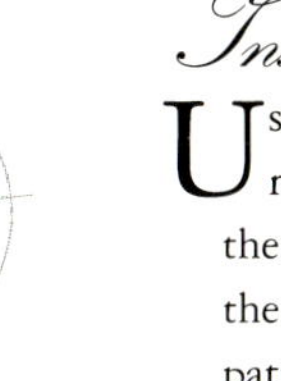

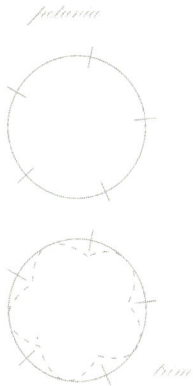

Instructions

Use the pattern as a guide, make a paper template to fit each size of cake, making sure that the points on the sides almost touch the board. Draw the parallel lines on to the template as shown. Marzipan and sugarpaste the cakes and leave to dry. Use the template to mark the outline of the pattern and then prick through to mark where the parallel lines cross. Remove template. Further define each pin prick with a modelling tool to make a small eyelet. Embroider the design by piping the lines, outlining the eyelets and piping tiny leaves with No.0 tube. Place gelatine droplets on the edge of the design. Pipe a row of small bulbs to neaten the join between cake and board.

Make petunias, clematis, pinks, blossoms and honeysuckle. Arrange in position on the cakes.

Gelatine Drops

30ml cold water and 2 level teaspoons gelatine power. Sprinkle gelatine on to cold water and soak. Dissolve over a gentle heat. Use a medicine dropper, suck up the liquid and make small drops on to a sheet of roasting bag paper. Use when dry.

Alison Proctor became interested in sugarcraft in 1982 when she realised that she could copy her favourite subject matter - plants - in three dimensional form. She has a great love of drawing and painting and is a member of the Society of Botanical Artists, and is a Judge and Demonstrator for the British Sugarcraft Guild.

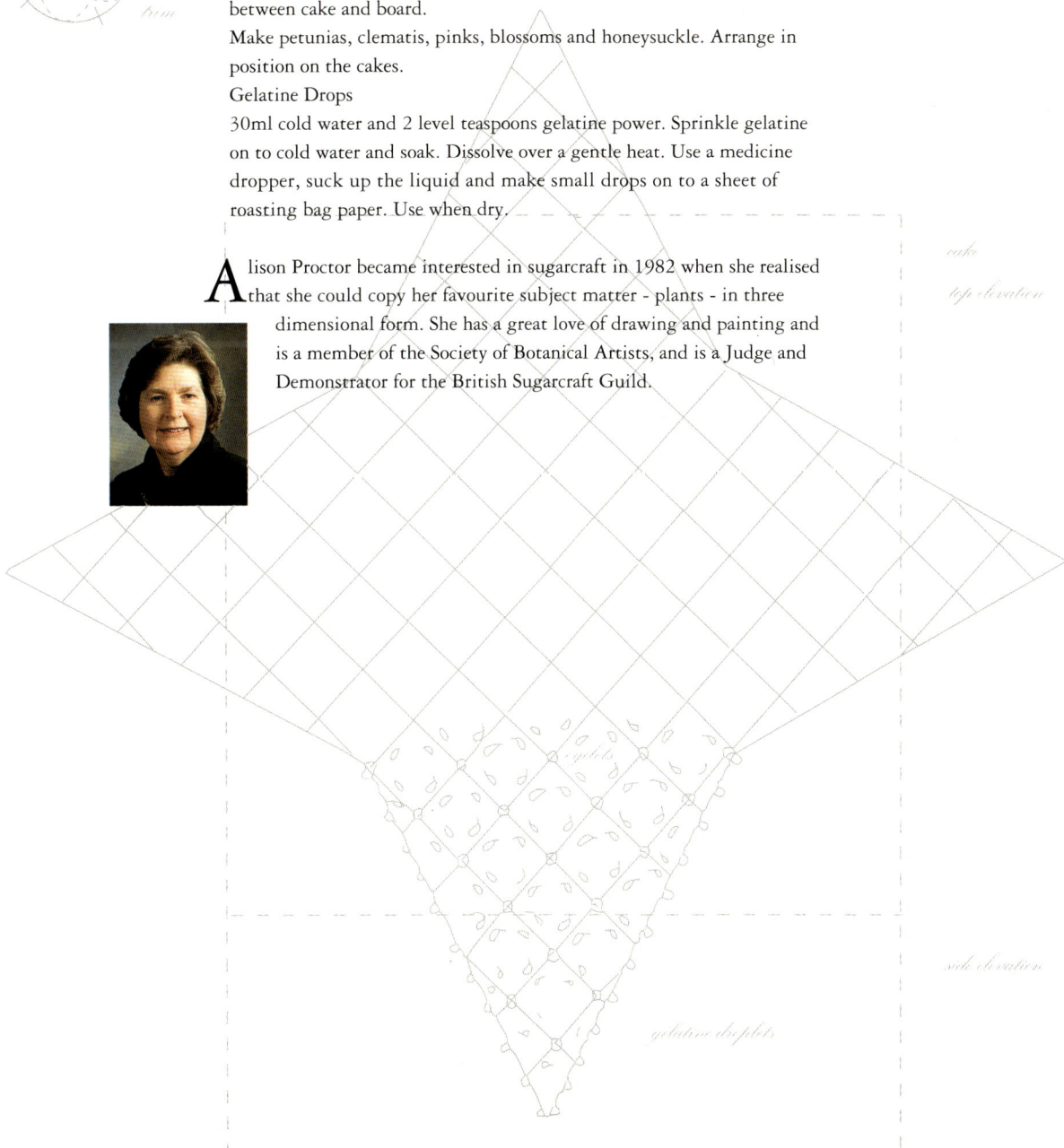

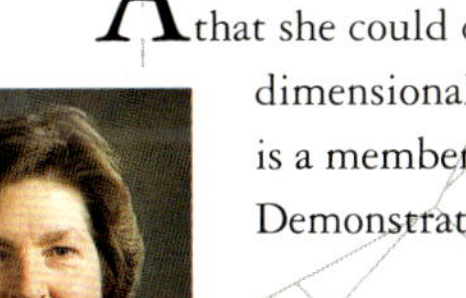

Crocus

CROCUS

BREAKTHROUGH Breast Cancer has a crocus for its logo and whilst experimenting with shape I found that by cutting from an oval cake I could obtain the shape of the crocus and achieve a very unusual tiered cake. The two side cakes were placed off set and the centre one lifted to give movement and natural feel to the overall effect.

Instructions

Using the template cut the shapes from an oval fruit cake. Coat each in marzipan. To add realism pad out the top of the crocus cake with a layer of sugarpaste to give the appearance of front and back petals, smoothing the joins. Coat all the cakes and boards with a layer of sugarpaste and leave to dry.For the extension work, turn the cake upside down on to a pad of foam sponge and mark the pattern at regular intervals with a pin. Using a No.00 tube pipe a loop from point 1 to pin at 2. When dry turn the cake the right way up and complete the loop to 3. Pipe the under loop from 1 to 3. When dry, pipe extension lines from top to bottom loop.The crocus and leaf design on the side of the cake is worked in brush embroidery.Make the crocuses and leaves and arrange on the cake. To complete scatter some sugarpaste pebbles on the board.

Janet North has an all consuming passion - sugarcraft! Consequently, she also has a very supportive and long suffering family. Janet has been teaching cake decoration for six years and has recently passed City and Guilds 7900 Creative Studies Course. She is currently studying Part II. She particularly enjoys making finely detailed miniature work.

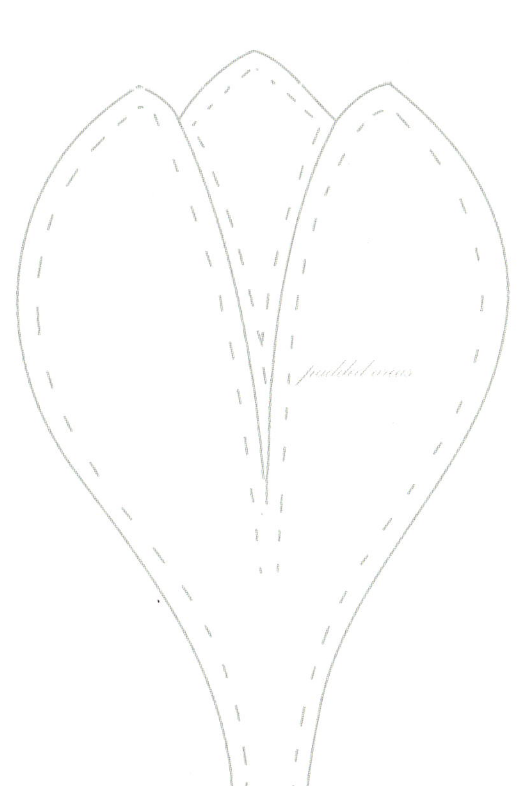

greased pin

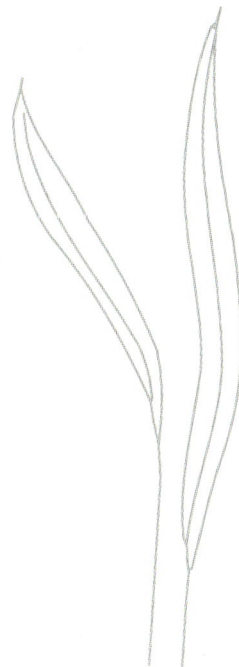

Techniques: Relief work 3, Brush embroidery, Extension work, Flowers

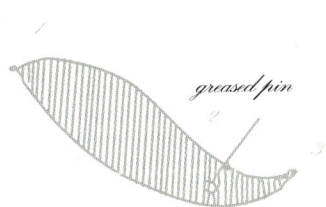

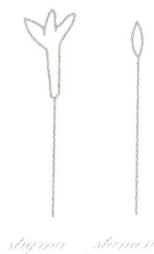

Divali

DIWALI

Diwali is a main festival of Hindus. It is the Festival of Lights. Traditionally people decorate their houses with oil lamps made of earthenware. These lamps are lit with oil and twigs. The design for the cake board is taken from one of the very popular Rajastani fabric designs.

Instructions

Coat a square cake drum in coloured sugarpaste. Cut a sheet of paper the same size as the drum and fold as shown in diagram 1. Mark the squares on to the sugarpaste. Copy the pattern to size as shown in diagram 2 and mark the pattern into the square areas using a pin.

Use a small metal rose petal cutter to cut the sugarpaste as shown and remove the sugarpaste to create a hole. Fill these holes with softened royal icing coloured green, yellow or white. Pipe the small squares with a No.1 tube using yellow, white and green royal icing.

Cut the lamp and flame from a cake as shown, marzipan and sugarpaste. Pipe the pattern on to the lamp cake. Make the small petals with softened royal icing on wax paper and when dry, fix in position as shown. The flame cake is finished with small petal shapes cut from sugarpaste, attached as shown and finally dusted with gold. Arrange the cakes in position on the cake board. Happy Diwali!

Born in Nasik, India, Anjali Rege obtained a degree in Law and Economics from Poona University. Anjali is married with two children and has been living in England since 1987. She joined the 7900 course at Brooklands and hopes to be able to teach in the future.

Techniques: Embroidery, Inlay

Dove

DOVE

BREAKTHROUGH Breast Cancer produced a book of information about the charity when it was first formed. The book featured many attractive and evocative photographs, one of which was a dove being released by a pair of captive hands. In the background are clouds. I designed and made this cake very soon after Jackie and I decided to compile this book.

Instructions

Place a 6" (15cm) cake (or dummy) on a round cake drum (10") 25cm and coat both cake and board in pale blue royal icing.Make the curved runout clouds, using royal icing coloured pale blue and white and blending the two together, and dry over the curve of a cake tin. Runout the bird head, including the dotted section on the design, which is the supporting area for the body.Prepare curved supports and using white, softened royal icing, pipe a line, following the lines on the template. Using a No.3 paintbrush, mark the icing through the line to create a feathered effect. Repeat this action with each line piped. Make sure all the lines are joined together and that there are no weak points. Dry well. Pipe a row of dots or small bulbs at the base edge.Stick all runouts in place with soft royal icing. Complete the design with strips of curled floristry ribbon.

The cake may be mounted on to another cake drum which has been coated in royal icing. For greater effect the cake can be offset on this supporting board.

Chris Jeffcoate

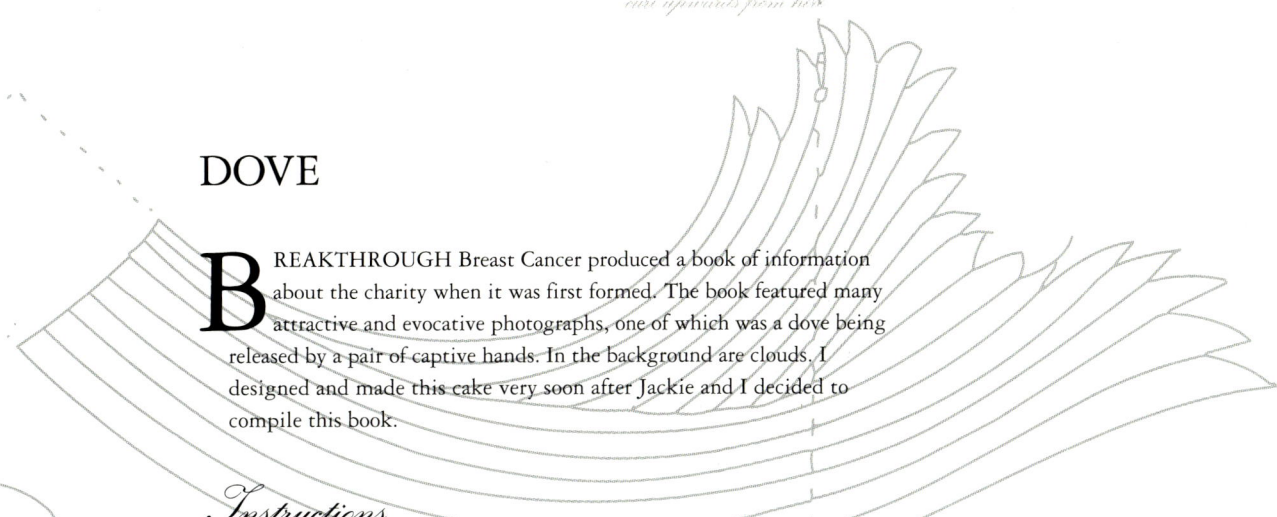

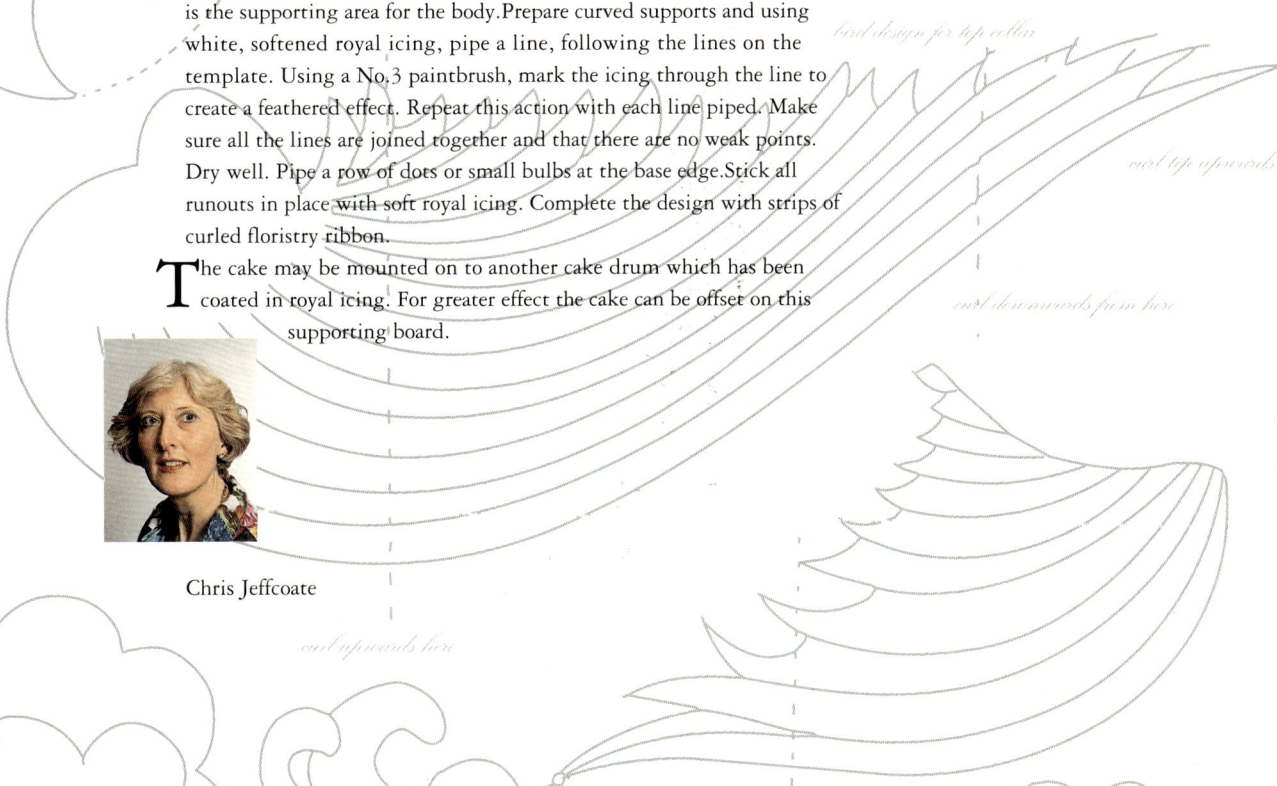

Techniques: Runouts, Pressure piping

Dragon Castle

DRAGON CASTLE

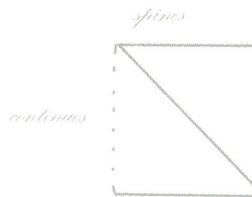

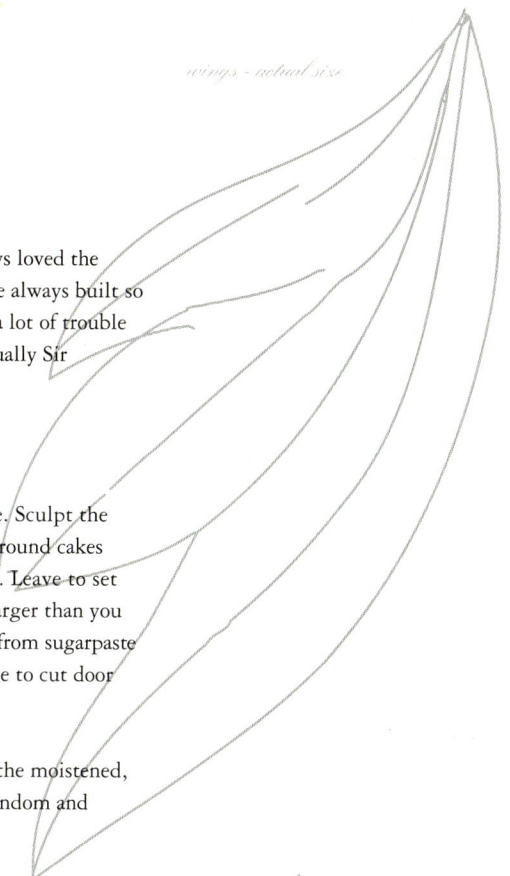

Dragons are always supposed to be lucky.I have always loved the myths and legends about King Arthur. Castles were always built so that they were easy to defend. King Pellinore had a lot of trouble with a dragon and spent most of his life chasing it. Eventually Sir Lancelot killed it for him - so the story goes.

Instructions

Use heavy genoese or fruit cake for the bases of this cake. Sculpt the base rock from a square slab and marzipan it and three round cakes (8",6",4") 20cm, 15cm, 10cm and set on thin cake cards. Leave to set before stacking all together.Paint the black spyholes on larger than you need them and mark the position of the door.Make a cone from sugarpaste for the top of the tower and glue in position. Use template to cut door from grey sugarpaste and fix in position.

Roll small balls of marbled sugarpaste and press them on the moistened, marzipanned walls of the structure, keeping the colours random and exposing the painted spyholes.

Use coloured royal icing and pastry brush to create textured rocks and cliffs on the base cake. Sponge green royal icing over the top of the 'cliffs' as grass.Make rock sugar (recipes) and glue around base of cake with green, blue and white royal icing to form waves breaking over the rocks.

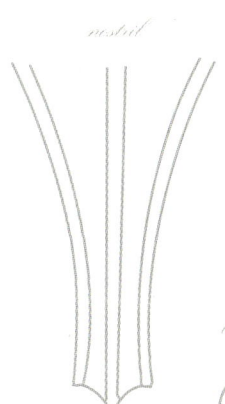

Top of tower is made by modelling sugarpaste to a 'crown' shape and covering with overlapping sugarpaste tiles. Make the dragon with modelling marzipan (recipes) using the drawings and photograph as a guide, building it in position on the cake.

Sue Haskell's first encounter with Brooklands College and sugarcraft was as a student. She is now a member of the support staff in the sugarcraft section and teaches part-time in Adult Education.

Designed in memory of Marianne Neald, another victim of Breast cancer, and sadly missed by all her sugarcraft friends.

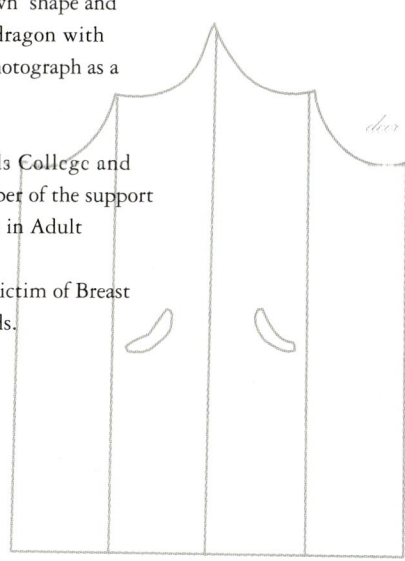

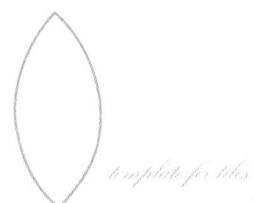

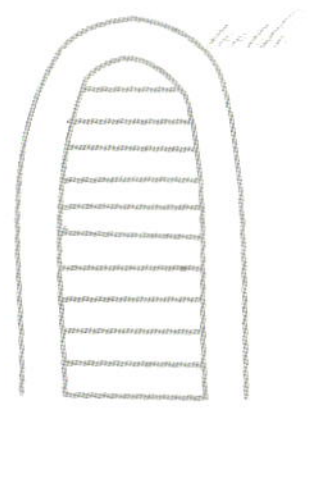

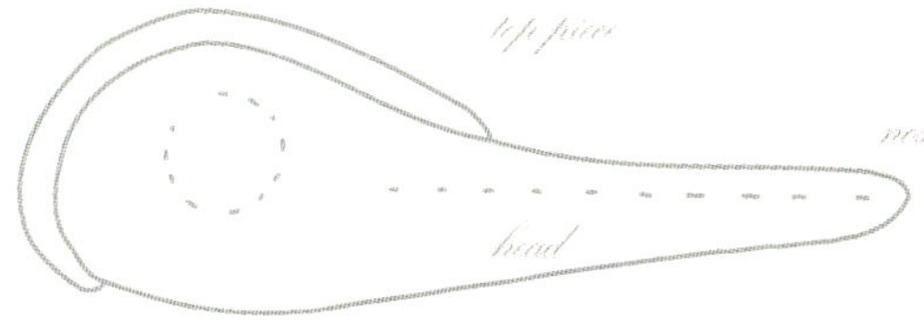

Fairies

FAIRIES

Inspiration for this cake came from imagining an archway covered in climbing honeysuckle - a background for a small world of fairies talking to the insects.

Instructions

Make a paper template the same size as an oval fruit cake and cut as shown in diagram. The larger section stands upright and the smaller section remains flat, on a scalloped oval board. Marzipan the back of the large cake first and allow to dry.

When dry, lay the marzipan side down on greaseproof paper to protect and coat top and sides in one layer. Join sides and back together smoothly. Coat small cake in the normal way. When dry, sugarpaste by the same method. Allow the cakes to harden well before applying the decoration.

Lay the large cake face down on a sheet of foam sponge. Enlarge and trace the monogram on the back of the cake and pressure pipe design. Pipe a suitable border pattern around the edge to cover the sugarpaste join. Dry well. Trace the fairies on to the front face and brush embroider and pressure pipe the design. The small cake has the monogram pressure piped on the front. Position the cakes on the marbled board.

Rosemary MacDonald has studied sugarcraft for six years, has recently started teaching and is an accredited demonstrator for the British Sugarcraft Guild. Rosemary is studying for the City and Guilds 7900 Creative Studies course at Brooklands.

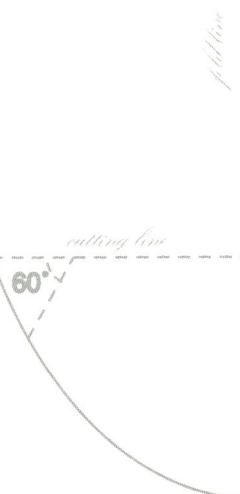

Techniques: Modelling, Pressure piping, Brush embroidery, Flowers

Flickering Candle

FLICKERING CANDLE

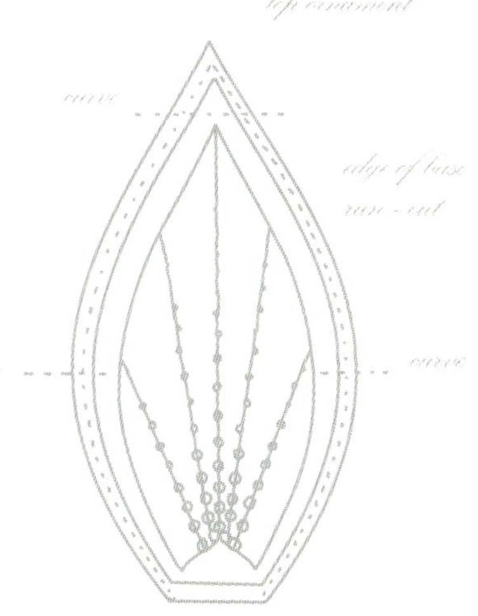

English cathedral architecture was my inspiration for this cake. The idea for the petal shaped runouts stems from the beams of a cathedral ceiling. They swept around in a symmetrical pattern and in the centre of each set of beams was a circular pattern very similar to petals forming a blossom, consequently suggesting my source for the brush embroidered sprays.

Colour was an important consideration, I chose grey as the base to represent the stone of the cathedral, adding a touch of blue to give a softer colour. Pink compliments the grey and represents the pink blossom. White gives highlights and lightens the overall effect.

By curling the runouts I was able to create a new dimension to the shape of the cake and by angling some I created the feeling of movement, like flames flickering in a breeze. I was pleased by the effect I created. I hope you like it too.

Instructions

Make two round fruit cakes and sandwich together with a layer of white almond paste, cover the cake with almond paste ensuring straight sides and a good ninety degree angle.Coat in royal icing.

Make the formers for the runouts and following the techniques instructions, make all the runouts and plenty of spares.

Place the side design on to the cake using the brush embroidery technique. The runout panels are then stuck in place with firm royal icing and sealed with a row of dots or small bulbs. Secure with props of soft sponge or cloud until the icing sets. Complete the design with fine linework following the line the runouts have made.

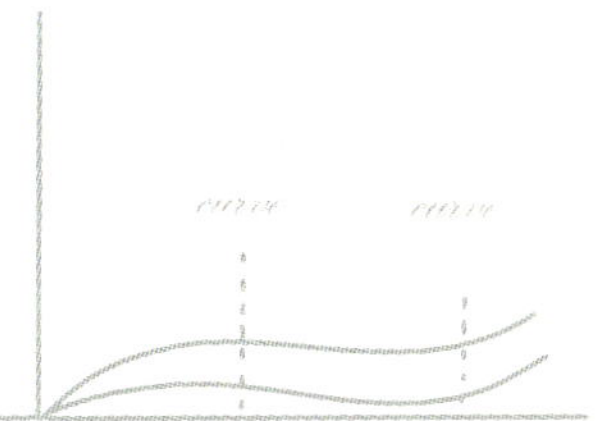

Chris Jeffcoate

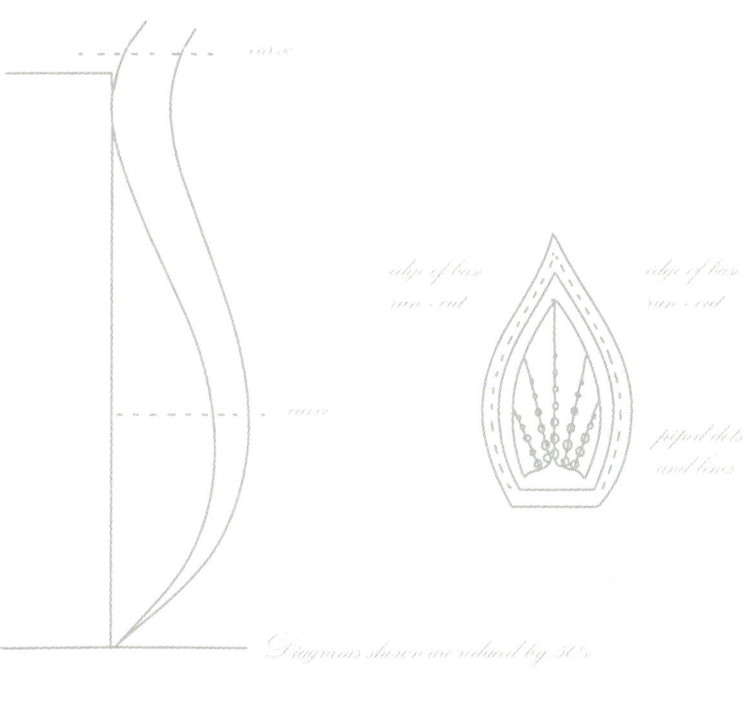

Techniques: Royal Icing - coating, Brush embroidery, Runouts

French Lace

FRENCH LACE

This cake started with a piece of Alencon lace and an idea from an hexagonal cake I had made about a year ago.

Instructions

Both cakes are 6" (15cm) high at the back and 3" (7.5cm) high at the front. Achieve this by sandwiching two oval cakes together with almond paste (for each tier) and slicing the top away before coating in almond paste.

Coat both cakes in a deep coloured royal icing, setting the bottom tier on an oval cake drum and the top tier on a round thick cake card. When dry trim the cake card to the shape and size of the top tier.

To marble, mix some icing whitener with water to the consistency of milk, dabbing and stroking this liquid on to the royal icing. I used a new pan scourer to apply it!

Make collars to fit the two sizes of cake using softened royal icing which will hold its shape and not require outlining. Fill in each part of the collar and allow to crust under a lamp before filling in the next section.

Transfer and complete the pressure piped pattern on the sides of the cake.Mark the collar pattern on the bottom cake drum and pressure pipe on direct.Pressure pipe the edge design and finally glue the collars in position with softened royal icing. Pipe a line of bulbs (No.1) between collars and cake edge to neaten.

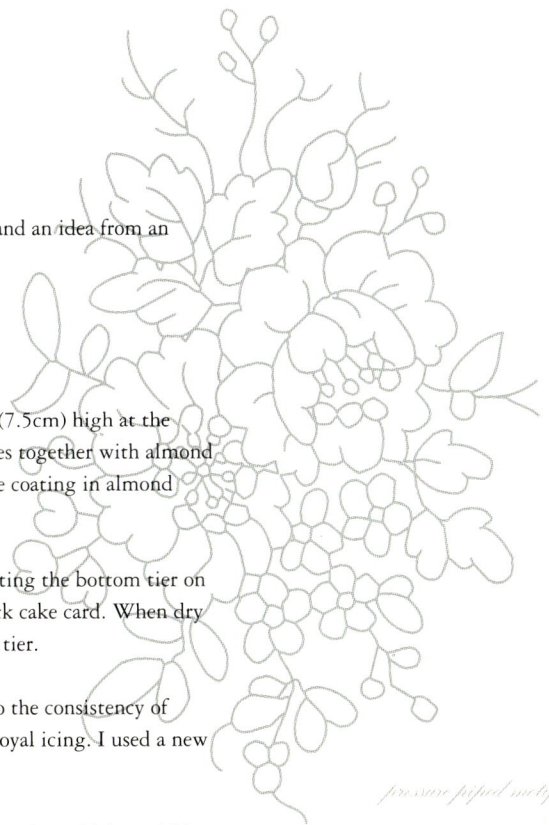

Jackie Kuflik

pressure piped motif

Collar (quarter sections)

side design

Techniques: Marbling, Pressure piping, Runouts

Winter

FOUR SEASONS WEDDING CAKES

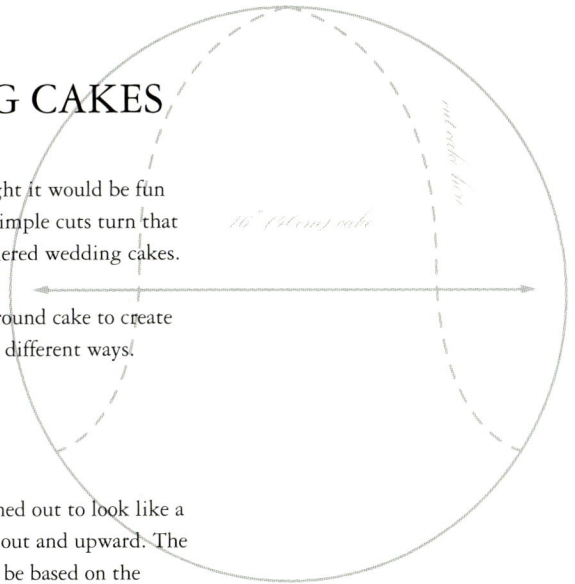

When creating this idea for the book, I thought it would be fun to take a basic shape and with one or two simple cuts turn that shape into exciting and original ideas for tiered wedding cakes.

The Four Seasons cakes have all been cut from a 16" round cake to create the common shape. This was then interpreted in four different ways.

WINTER

It was purely by accident that the shapes I had cut turned out to look like a snowdrop by just lifting the two symmetrical shapes out and upward. The whole theme of the winter wedding cake then had to be based on the snowdrop.

Instructions

Marzipan and sugarpaste the cakes. Glue a narrow green ribbon around the base of each cake. Use a mixture of sugarpaste and flowerpaste to make the pleated effect around the base of the cakes.
Make the lace on waxed paper with No.00 tube. Mark the sides of the cake evenly to prepare for the extension work. The loops are piped in No.00 tube with the cake tilted towards you so that the loops will not touch the cake side. Decorate with graduated dots and attach the lace.
To make the central decoration cut a base from gum paste following the shape of the cake at the back and any free-style at the front. Make a selection of winter flowers, snowdrops, crocuses, aconites, willow catkins and alder catkins. Make a selection of leaves from brown flowerpaste.
Glue some white sugarpaste to the base and whilst is it still soft arrange all the flowers in place. Scatter the brown leaves at the base of the display.
Spray a fine mist of water over the surface of the base of the arrangement and sprinkle with 'snow'

Chris Jeffcoate

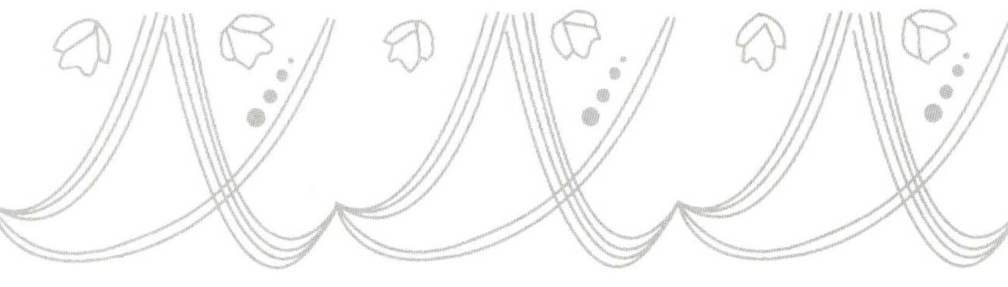

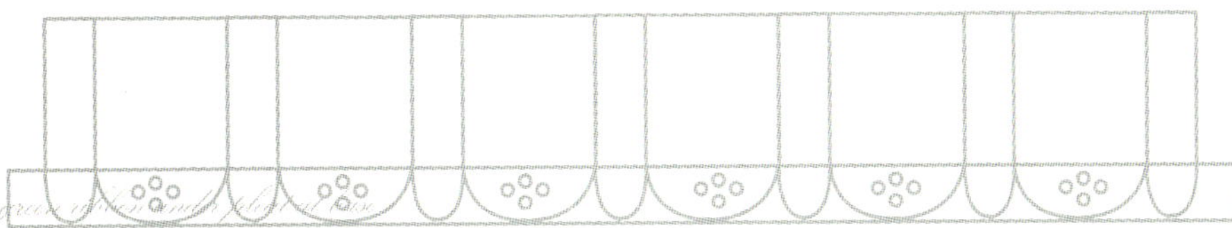

Techniques: Extension work, Lace, Pleating (2), Flowers, 'Snow'

Autumn

AUTUMN

This wedding cake has been designed to complement a bride's dress from an original design by Jenny Burgess. The neckline of the dress is embroidered with chrysanthemums, oak and corn and by coincidence the shape of the large cake resembles the back neckline of the dress.

Instructions

Marzipan and sugarpaste the cakes and boards.Secure a ribbon to the base of the cakes and pipe a line of bulbs with a No.1 tube alongside. Measure the circumference of the cakes and position the template for the extension work evenly around the cakes. Prick the pattern through and pipe small dots with No.0 tube as shown in the diagram. Tilt the turntable towards you and using a No.0 tube and royal icing, drop loops to begin the corn design. The loops should hang clear of the side of the cake. When dry, turn the cake over and rest on a pad of foam sponge, and with it tilting towards you again, drop loops to close the corn shape. When dry turn the cake back on its base, pipe the top 'ear' and stem of the corn. Make the chrysanthemums and arrange as shown on the cake.

corn design

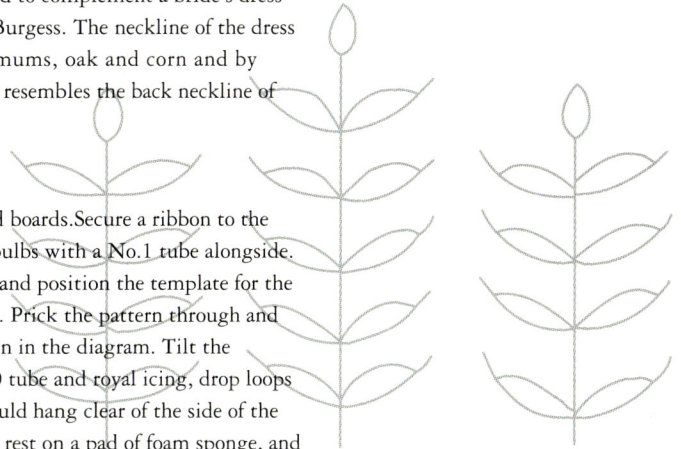

Chris Ganderton made her first wedding cake in 1987. "I had never had any lessons so I borrowed lots of cake decorating books from the library and lost a lot of sleep. The cake turned out quite well and was featured in a national magazine! I signed up for evening classes and did two years before braving Brooklands College and joined up for the C&G 7900. I completed the course in the Summer of '92 having lost lots more sleep". Chris is currently studying Part II at Brooklands and hoping for a cure for insomnia.

positioning of dots for corn design

templates for chrysanthemums

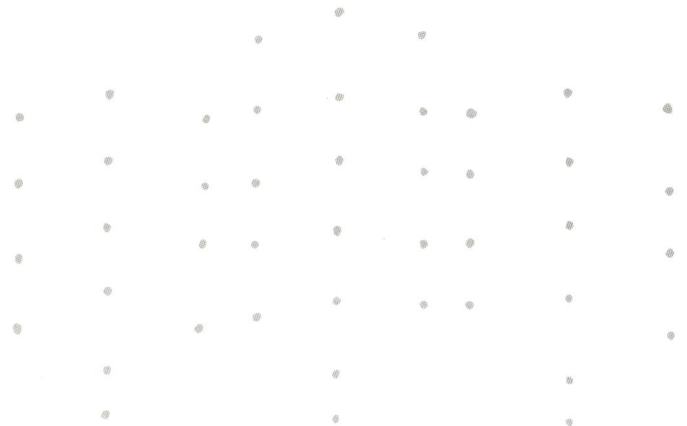

Techniques: Extension loops, Flowers

Spring

SPRING

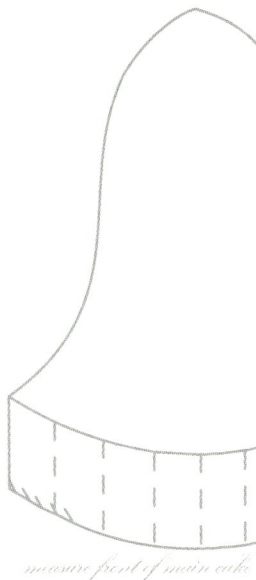

I have a beautiful lilac tree in my garden, Syringa Vulgaris, which, when it starts to blossom, assures me that Spring has arrived.

bell extension work pattern

measure front of main cake

Instructions

Marzipan and sugarpaste the cakes and boards. Allow to dry. Measure the front of the main cake evenly and scribe the top half of the bell pattern on. (Adjust the size of the template as required - we fitted 8 bell shapes on our cake) Pipe the bottom loop of the bell on to wax paper with a No.1 tube and leave to dry for six hours. Glue these very carefully on to the cake surface, matching the scribed shapes, with royal icing and leave to dry. These loops should stand out at 90° angle to the cake side. Mark the top line of the second extension work pattern on to the other sides of the cakes and put greased pins in place for the bottom line. Pipe all the embroidery on to the cakes with No.00 tube. Drop loops on the pins and leave to dry. Pipe all vertical extension lines as shown on both patterns.Pipe linework around the top edge of each tier with No.0 tube.Make the lilac, arrange and fit to cake as shown.

When June Amos saw the christening cake that had been made for her daughter Susan she decided that she wanted to try cake decorating for herself. She has been teaching in Adult Education since 1973 in East and South Kent and is currently studying Part II at Brooklands.

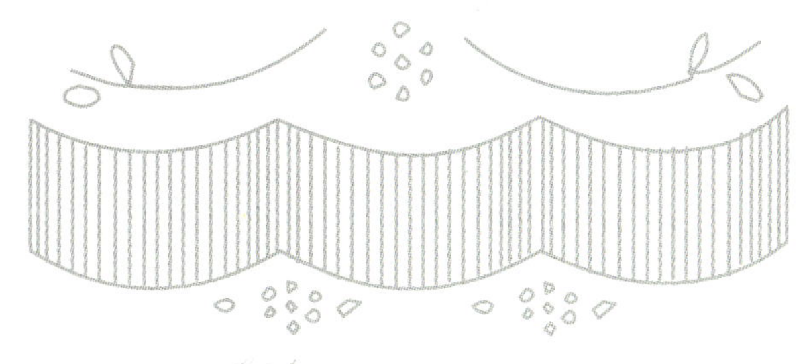

second extension work pattern

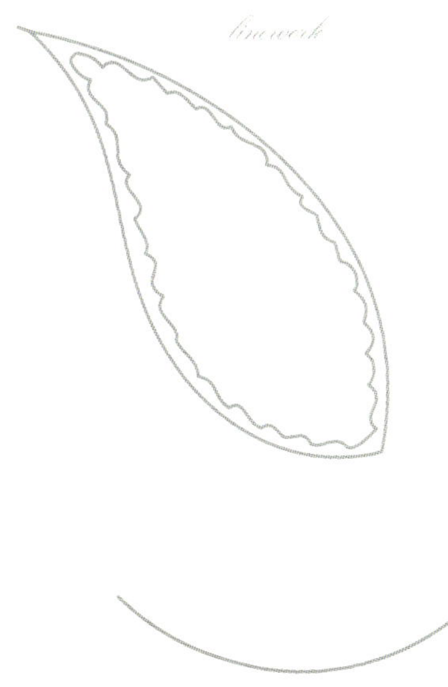

Techniques: Extension work, Embroidery, Flowers

Summer

SUMMER

The design for this cake was taken from the design on the sleeves of a bridal gown.

Instructions

Marzipan and sugarpaste the cakes and boards. With No.1 tube, pipe the bridgeless extension loop over pins along the front edge of the base cake only.

When complete and dry drop extension lines down using a No.00 tube. Pipe three loops over the top of the extension work with No.0 tube and continue this 3 loop pattern all the way round the sides of the base cake. The 3 loop pattern is repeated on the smaller side cakes with the pattern starting low at the front and finishing at the top of the cake at the pointed end. Ensure that the loops are piped in a perfectly horizontal line at all times which will mean having to tilt the cake accordingly. Brush embroider the alstroemeria design on to the top of both side cakes.

Make some small flowerpaste horseshoes and attach to the cake where required. Make the alstroemeria and the small 'mexican hat method' filler flowers, arrange on the cake as shown.

Dorothy Holmes first cake was for her daughters' wedding and she had already made the wedding outfit! Since then, some eight years ago, 'Dot' has travelled to Australia and South Africa to visit their National Sugarcraft Exhibitions and made many friends. She completed the 7900 Part I at Brooklands and has returned to study Part II.

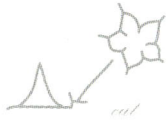

Techniques: Extension work, Brush embroidery, Flowers

Garden Wall

GARDEN WALL

The idea for the cake came from a gardening book that had an archway through which distant hills could be seen. I think this would make a lovely retirement or house-warming cake.

Instructions

Marzipan and coat cake and board in white royal icing. Cut out the clouds and hills and use these as a mask for airbrushing the top of the cake blue for the sky.Use a small artists palette knife and coloured royal icing to create the hills.

Make a runout of the cottage and when dry position on cake, adding bushes and trees in rough royal icing. Use template to produce 'brick wall' top and bottom runout collars. Leave to dry and secure to cake. Add a selection of leaves made from flowerpaste, bushes from marzipan (pushed through a sieve) and pebbles from sugarpaste.

Celia Collins makes delicious cakes and has now joined Brooklands to learn how to decorate them, attending the C&G 7900 course.

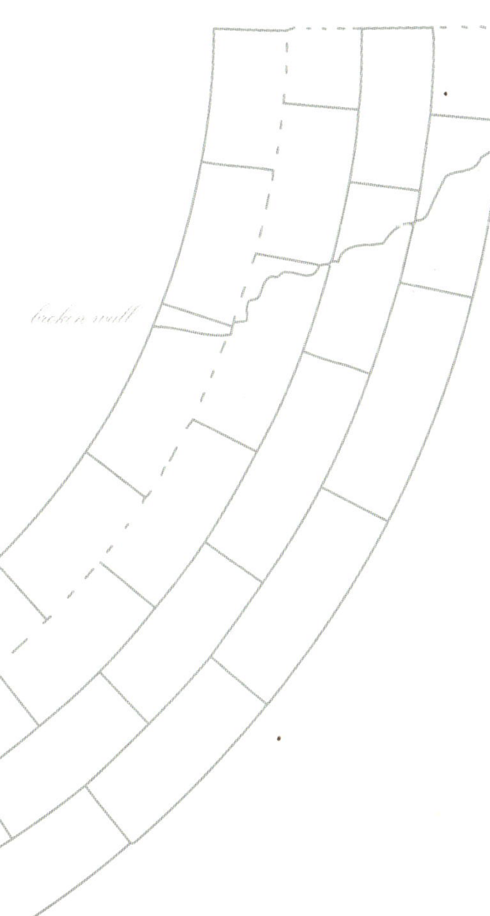

edge of top collar

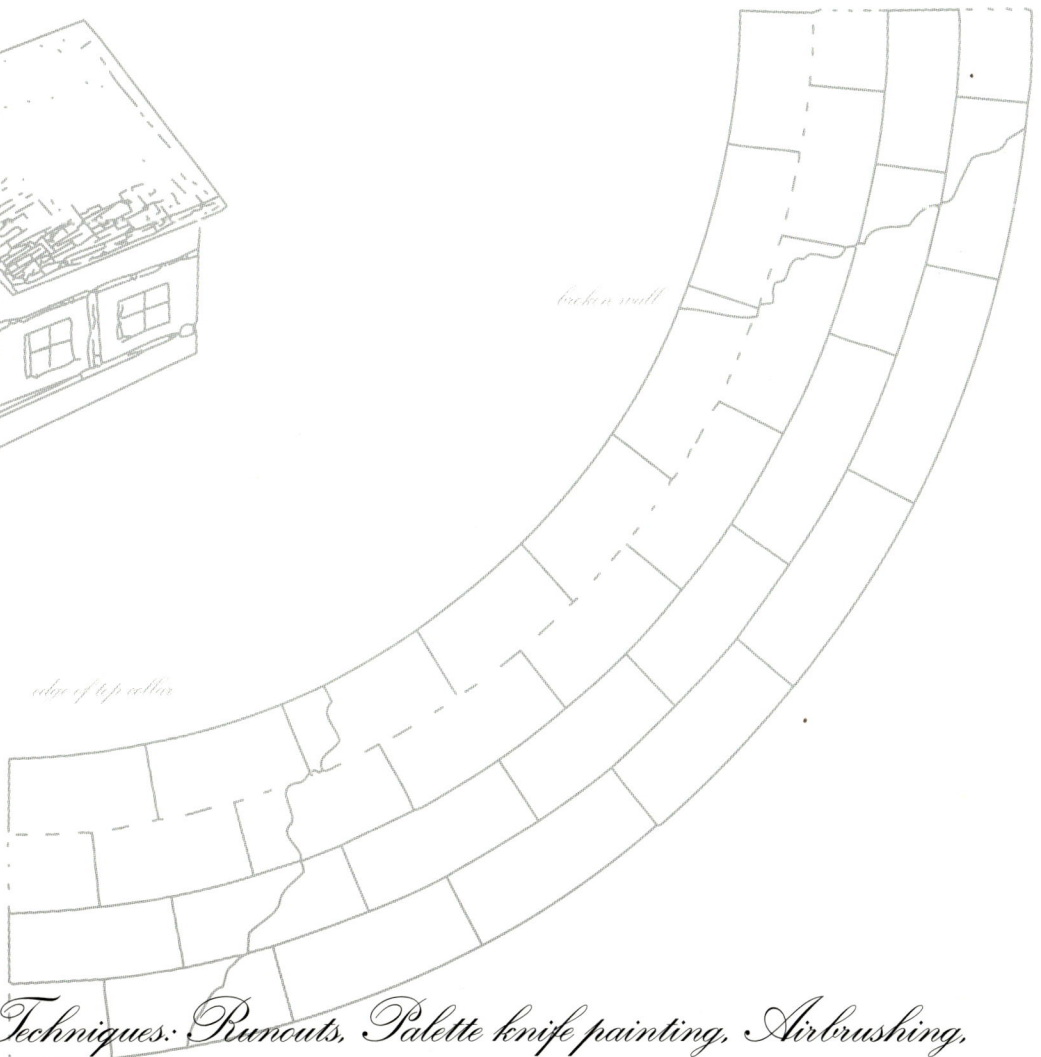

Techniques: Runouts, Palette knife painting, Airbrushing.

Geese

Holly cutter (actual size)

GEESE

My inspiration for this cake was taken from a class visit to the Victoria and Albert Museum where I made detailed sketches of a decorative "festive" wood carving. It lent itself very directly to reproduction in carved fruit cake and modelled sugarpaste.

Instructions

You will need a large shallow fruit cake and we suggest baking a 10" (25cm) round mixture in a 12" round tin. Enlarge the template to fit a 12" (30cm) circle and cut two copies. Use one template to cut out the fruit cake to the basic shape. Thin down the birds heads and necks and the grass blades slightly to allow for application of marzipan and sugarpaste. Coat the sides and then the top in marzipan ensuring you smooth all the joins well.

Cut the second template out into various sections like a jigsaw puzzle. Use these sections to mark round and form the relief design. Indent grass blades and build up the marzipan wreath and wing.

Sugarpaste the cake section by section, shaping and modelling as you go before the paste has time to crust. Use modelling tools to create the carved effects and textures. Make and apply the holly leaves and berries and tufts of grass around the birds' feet.

When dry, paint the birds beaks and highlights on the wreath and grass with edible gold (or apply gold leaf). Paint in all details and finally create 'antiqued' look with beige colouring, and accentuate carved effect with black and grey colouring. Coat and texture the board in mixture of blue, green and white royal icing to give the effect of snow falling.

Jo Acres iced cakes 'from when she was little' and decided to "learn the skills properly" by taking 7900. Previous to this she had studied art, design and teaching at Oxford Polytechnic. Jo now works in a specialist medical library and takes 'the odd cake commission alongside".

Geese template (shown reduced by 50%)

Geisha

GEISHA

I was inspired to make the Japanese Lady at a short course with Terri Mansell at Brooklands. It fascinated me and, as I had done very little bas relief work, it was a real challenge.

Instructions

Using the template cut the shape from a 10" (25cm) round cake. Marzipan and sugarpaste the cake and a 12" (30cm) cake drum in the usual way. Transfer the flower motif to the surface and brush embroider in colours as shown.

Trace the drawings of the hands and face and make in runout royal icing or pressure piping on waxed paper. Allow to dry. Make the under support for the lady with sugarpaste and position. Using a mixture of sugarpaste and flowerpaste dress the lady. Dress and apply her arms separately. Make a fan, with the template, and slightly frill the edges. Fix the hands in place and add the fan. The face should be attached and the join covered by the collar of the dress. Finish by handpainting all features and royal icing the hair with a No.1 tube.

To make the fans for the border, start with a dark purple flowerpaste, roll out paste and cut 3 fans. Frill rounded edge with a cocktail stick. Add a pea size piece of white paste and mix to produce a paler tone, cut 3 more. Continue in this way until you have 18 different tones (plus extras for breakages). Allow to dry and paint edges with edible gold. Place the fans in position using royal icing. Make and position the fantasy Japanese flowers.

Louise Prescott's introduction to cake decorating was at an Adult Education course for basic icing. After the first lesson she was fascinated and 'hooked' and feels fortunate in having had an inspiring tutor in Jean Seagrave. Louise is studying City and Guilds 7900 Creative Studies Course at Brooklands and enjoying every minute! Louise is a violin teacher and finds that the contrast of cake decorating is both relaxing and rewarding.

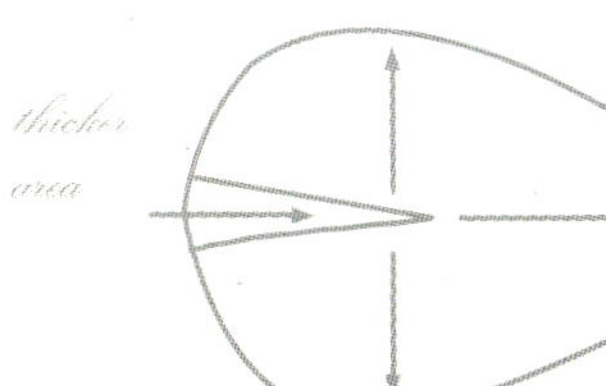

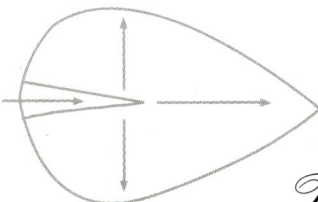

Techniques: Brush embroidery, Relief work 4, Flowers

Honesty

HONESTY

My inspiration came from the shapes I was experimenting with. I thought that Honesty was an interesting seed head to make and I reflected its colour in the coating of the cakes.

Instructions

Cut the cakes as shown in the diagram. Marzipan and sugarpaste all cakes, setting cakes 1 and 2 on thin cake cards and cake 3 on its prepared board. When set pipe the bridgeless extension work and embroidery on to the sides of the cake, turning the cake over as necessary on to a piece of foam sponge. Cut the large board as shown and cover in sugarpaste, glueing around the outside edge only. Make a paper template of cakes 1 and 2, position on the large board where required, cut out and remove the sugarpaste shapes. Remove the thin cake cards carefully and set the cakes into position. Seal the edge with a row of piped bulbs. [N.B. This method ensures a smooth coating for the board and a very clean join between cake and board. We recommend only this method and never place fruit cakes directly on to any sugarpaste] Make flowers and seed heads, arrange in position on the cake.

A soft furnisher by trade, Lynn Wright took up porcelain modelling and cake decorating as a hobby five years ago. She embarked on the City and Guilds 7900 Creative Studies Course which she completed in a year together with her teaching certificate. Her enthusiasm and dedication won her the recognition of Student of the Year 91/92 giving her the confidence to teach and share all the pleasures of sugarcraft.

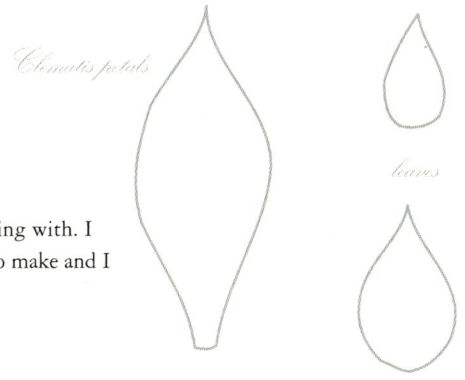

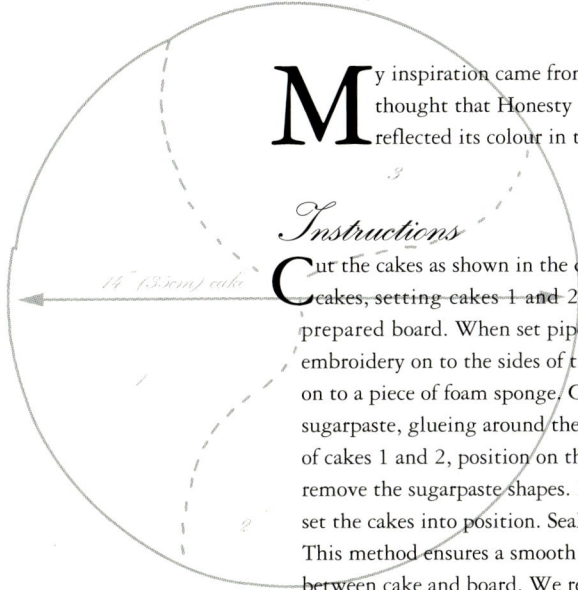

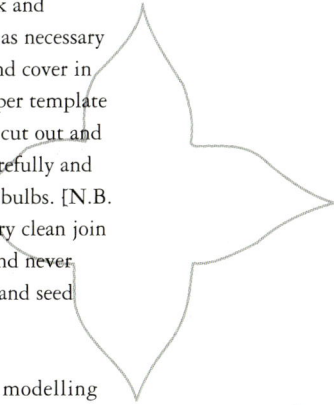

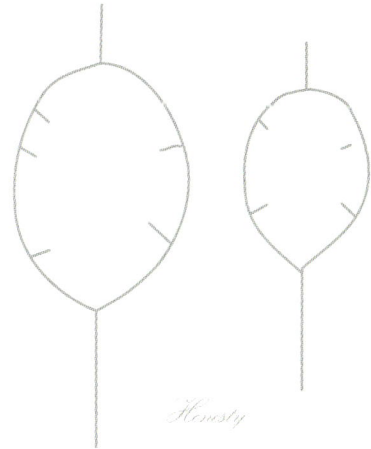

Clematis petals

leaves

14" (35cm) cake

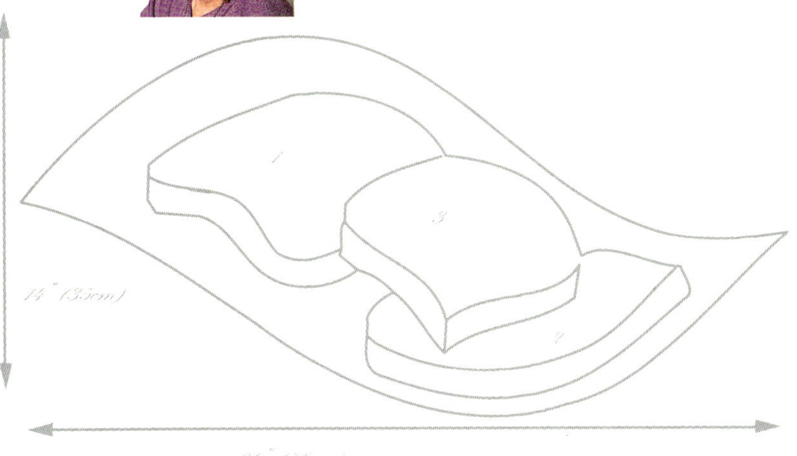

Honesty

Extension Work and Embroidery
pipe from the cake to the pin and back on to the cake. For bottom loop angle the cake forward then pipe loop touching at the cake edge (allow to dry before moving on)

Techniques: Extension work, Embroidery, Flowers

Horse

HORSE

It is always difficult to think of a subject for a mans cake but many men are interested in horse racing and I think horses are the most beautiful of creatures so maybe this idea will inspire you.

Instructions

Prepare an 8" (20cm) round cake on 12" (30cm) round cake drum, marzipan and coat in royal icing.Make the runout collar and leave to dry for at least 24 hours. Cut out the template of the horse head from stencilling paper and using an airbrush, build up a design of horses running a race around the sides of the cake, using at least three shades of green food colouring.

Prepare the motif of the horse and jockey using pressure piping method or runout method on waxed paper. Place the collar on the cake and fix the horse over the top with soft royal icing.

Make a white fence in pastillage and glue in position with royal icing and support if necessary with foam sponge or cloud until dry. Complete with small flowerpaste daisies and dried flowers fixed in position with a little royal icing.

Leanne Buckerfield studied Art and Graphic Design at Kingston and went on to work in a Graphic Design Agency in London. Her training drew her back to glass engraving and then on to study creative sugarcraft at Brooklands College.

Runout collar

Template for airbrushing

Motif of horse and jockey

Techniques: Airbrushing, Runouts, Pressure piping

Indian Palace

INDIAN PALACE

I found the original idea (the Taj Mahal) whilst looking through holiday brochures. With further research I found some interesting balustrades which I incorporated into the collars. The water effects, reflections and ripples, I have represented in the airbrushing techniques and by scoring the surface of the royal icing.

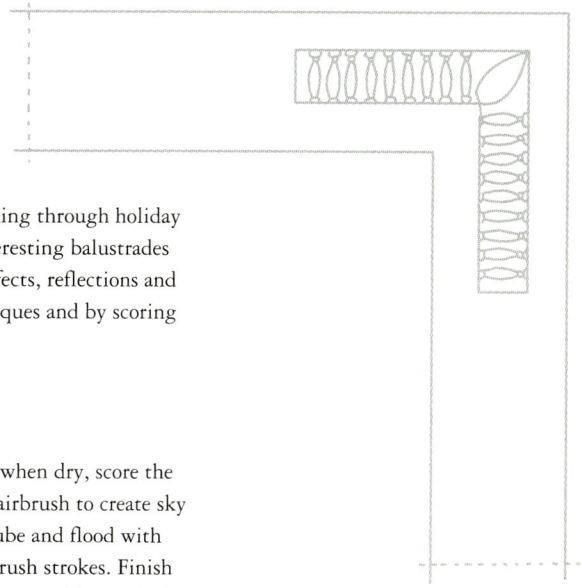

Instructions

Coat an 8" (10cm) square cake with royal icing and when dry, score the top. Coat a 12" (30cm) square cake drum. Use an airbrush to create sky and water effect. Outline central motif with No.0 tube and flood with softened royal icing. The reflection is added using brush strokes. Finish by adding turrets with No.1 tube. Make top and bottom collars and when dry pipe balustrades on top collar only.

Fix bottom collar to the board and then pipe the balustrades in position. Attach cake. Make four side designs with runout icing and when dry airbrush with a little yellow colour. Make the squares for the raised areas - 4 of each size.

Pipe 3,2,1,linework on the sides of the cake using the template. Pipe large and small bulbs between cake and bottom collar with No.2 and No.3 tubes to neaten join. Attach side designs. Assemble and attach the raised areas to the sides of both top and bottom collar. Finally, place top collar into position and attach. Pipe small plain bulbs (No.1) under the top collar to neaten the join between collar and cake top.

Marion Pryke has been studying sugarcraft for nine years and is now attending the 7900 Creative Studies Course at Brooklands. She enjoys crafts of all kinds.

Techniques: Runouts, Scoring, Airbrush.

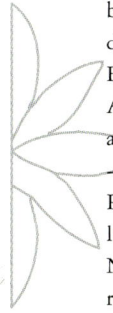

Kings Road

KINGS ROAD

A chance visit to the King's Road, Chelsea, left me fascinated by all the different fashions, characters and personalities of the people in the street. I chose three types of punk to represent some of the many individuals I saw. Afro Punk - relaxed, happy, self assured individuals, Designer Punk - well heeled people who wanted to appear punk but were drawn towards expensive, individually designed versions of punk leather, Traditional Punk - young, intensely independent creative people, constantly adding new variations to the punk image.

This cake will take a long time to make. There is not enough space here to give step-by-step instructions but we offer you hints and tips of making some of the features and instructions for building the basic form. We advise the study of photographs, magazine pictures, anatomy, etc., as well as your own face in a mirror, not only to understand the structure but how the face moves and changes shape with different expressions. Build the whole structure in the base cake, use boiled jam to cover small sections at a time with marzipan. Finally, 'dress' the marzipan coating with various sugars.

Moulding faces

The structure is built up using small pieces of marzipan and then laying a thin skin (of sugarpaste or a mix of sugarpaste and flowerpaste) over the whole face and neck in one application. To keep the face soft and workable over a period of time, keep a plastic bag over it between sessions. Pay attention to bone structures, eye sockets, the nose, etc. checking the profile as you go. Finally, make sure you have the right expression on the face and that the surface is as smooth as possible before applying the skin (a thin sheet of sugarpaste/flowerpaste).

Building up the face and head

Eyebrows and eyelashes are piped with No.1 tube, eyes painted.

Clothing - Make paper patterns to ease the cutting and fitting of clothes to the bodies, working on one area at a time, i.e. an arm or the collar. Studs are made by piping round bulbs of royal icing and stippling with white snowflake powder whilst still wet. Leave to dry before applying. Sweater textures can be produced by texturing with modelling tools or pressing on clean pieces of real knitting!

Hair - wet look. Mix three colours, one for the roots, one the 'last colour' and finally the most recent application. In that order spread these over the head and pull a narrow spatula (artists oil spatula 6mm) through the hair to reveal roots and create gel look. Tidy up by stroking with a skewer.

Hair - shaven. Press a mixture of sugarpaste and flowerpaste through a plastic tea strainer until short strands appear. Cut these away from the strainer and apply to the head.

Hair - tufted. Mix stripy paste (brown and tangerine), roll and apply.

Make templates to work out positioning of figures

Hair - Afro. To make it interesting to look at, this style will have many different shades of brown, be graded in length, vary in density and be arranged in clusters. Take a pea sized piece of flowerpaste, coloured brown, and roll into a tapered sausage 6cm long on a board dusted with brown dusting powder. Spiral this round a very lightly greased length of thin piano wire or florists stub wire and leave to partially dry. Apply to the head. The spiral should be soft enough to arrange in position but firm enough not to unwind. Further colouring will be required to give the hair movement.

Geraldine Dahlke graduated as a teacher in 1971 with a B.Ed(Hons) specialising in Art/Craft. She spent the next ten years in Primary Education, gaining an M.Ed and a Deputy Headship before giving up this career to begin a much delayed one as a spinner and weaver. Now married with two children, she began cake decorating when her children asked for novelty Birthday cakes. She is currently studying for the City and Guilds 7900 Creative Studies Course at Brooklands College.

Add a slice of cake to front of Designer Punk for stability

Techniques: Runouts, Sculpturing, Painting, Modelling

Lorraine

LORRAINE

The design for this cake was inspired by the tattoo I have on my right shoulder. I wanted to use strong, bright colours and I chose the name to dedicate the cake to my friend Lorraine so that she'll be reminded of our 'sugarcraft time' together.

Instructions

Prepare an 8" fruit cake for royal icing. Place on a 14" round cake drum and coat both the cake and the board in royal icing. Draw the outline of the bottom collar directly into position on the board and flood. Pipe the bulb pattern around the base of the cake.

Prepare the top collar by firstly running out the white band. The tree trunk, bird tail and wings, and the foliage around the tree are pressure piped in appropriate colours. The tree top is runout using three different shades of green, applied and mixed together at the same time. Leave to dry.

Mark 12 birds with template in equal spaces around the side of the cake and brush embroider in appropriate colours. Pipe freehand the trees, bushes and grass. Pressure pipe the tail theme and the bouquets of dots and leaves around the bottom collar as shown on the drawing. Pipe the name. Fix the top collar on to the cake top and pipe 2,1,0 linework around the birds tail.

Carmen Odgaard.

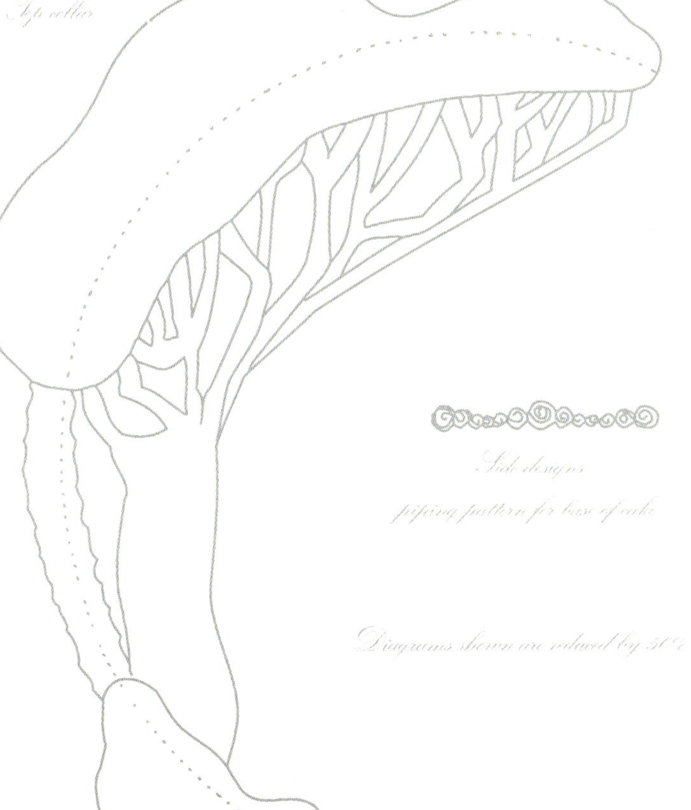

Side designs
piping pattern for base of cake

Diagrams shown are reduced by 50%

cake line

Techniques: Runouts, Pressure piping

Maori

MAORI

Having travelled from New Zealand to the UK to attend 7900 Creative Studies Course at Brooklands, I thought what better than to create a cake with a New Zealand theme. On the 6th February each year, New Zealanders celebrate their National Day to commemorate the signing of a treaty at Waitangi between the early settlers and the indigenous Maori people.

Instructions

Coat the cake in off-white royal icing. Coat a 12" (30cm) double thick board in royal icing, running the sugar down on to the edges of the board. When dry, mount this board on to a 10" round drum. (This protects the edge of the board). When the cake is dry, measure it carefully and make the top and bottom collars and the small over-runouts. Make 6 runouts for the side of the cake, drying each over a curved shape (the same size tin as the cake is ideal). Place cake on board but do not fix. Use an airbrush to create a dense colour on the board and fade out up the sides of the cake. When dry, remove cake, fix bottom collar in position, replace cake into position, attach small over-runouts and side runouts. Pressure pipe the figure on to the top of the cake. Finally, attach the top collar.Make Pohutakawa Flowers and arrange on cake.

Lesley Husband from Hamilton, New Zealand has had a long interest in sugarcraft and specialises in creating co-ordinated cakes for individual brides. Recently Lesley has widened her talents by combining floral art and water colour painting with her sugarcraft skills.

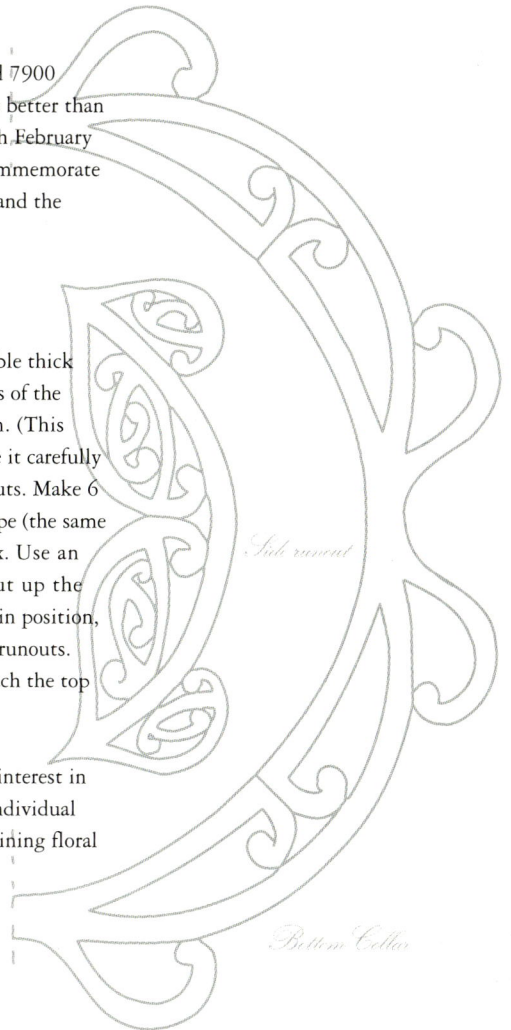

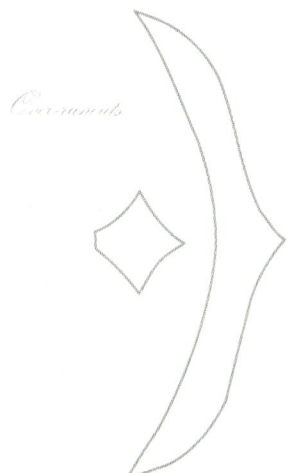

Techniques - Pressure Piping, Runout work, Flowers

Monet Bridge

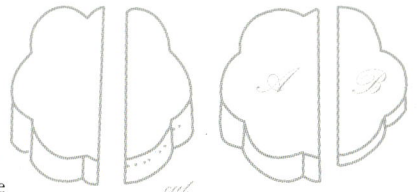

MONET BRIDGE

I recently visited Egham Swan Sanctuary and it was wonderful to get so close to the birds. Dot Beeson started the sanctuary with one swan. She has such a wonderful rapport with the birds some of which stay with her for life. You can only visit by appointment but it is well worth it and has a fabulous atmosphere. I then went to Paris and studied Monet's work. The colours, particularly in his painting of water and pools, together with his interpretation of waterlilies all combined to create the inspiration for this cake.

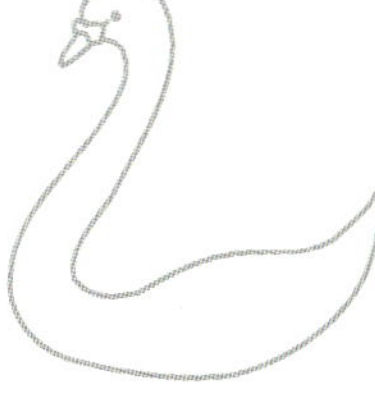

Instructions

Cut a petal shaped 3" (7.5cm) deep fruit cake as shown in step 1.Step 2 - split the depth of the smaller cake into 1" (2.5cm) deep and 2" (5cm) deep layers. You now have three cakes,(a) one large full depth,(b) one small 1" (2.5cm) depth and (c) one small 2" (5cm) depth from which you cut away the centre petal shape.Stand cake (a) on cut edge and marzipan both sides and along top edge. Stand cake (c) on cut edge directly in front of cake (a) and marzipan top edge and front. Keep cake (b) flat, push up to front of cake (c) and marzipan all exposed cake.

Make the bridge using a sheet of pastillage dried over one petal of the cake tin. Fix to cake (c). Sugarpaste all areas,including the bridge, panel by panel and smoothing all edges carefully. Coat the cake drums in sugarpaste and cover join between cake and drum with neatly rolled sausage of sugarpaste.

Make rails and posts for bridge in pastillage and leave to dry before assembly.Make backdrop of trees with sugarpaste branches and pressure piped royal icing leaves.Make the runout swans and leave to dry before glueing in position with royal icing. Support as necessary.Model flowers and swans and arrange on cake.

Terri Mansell (lecturer at Brooklands) has been involved in sugarcraft for at least 10 years and has taught in Adult Education. Terri has been with the Sugarcraft team at Brooklands for four years and brings with her a wealth of artistic talent, a gentle and caring nature and an OUTRAGEOUS attitude to life!

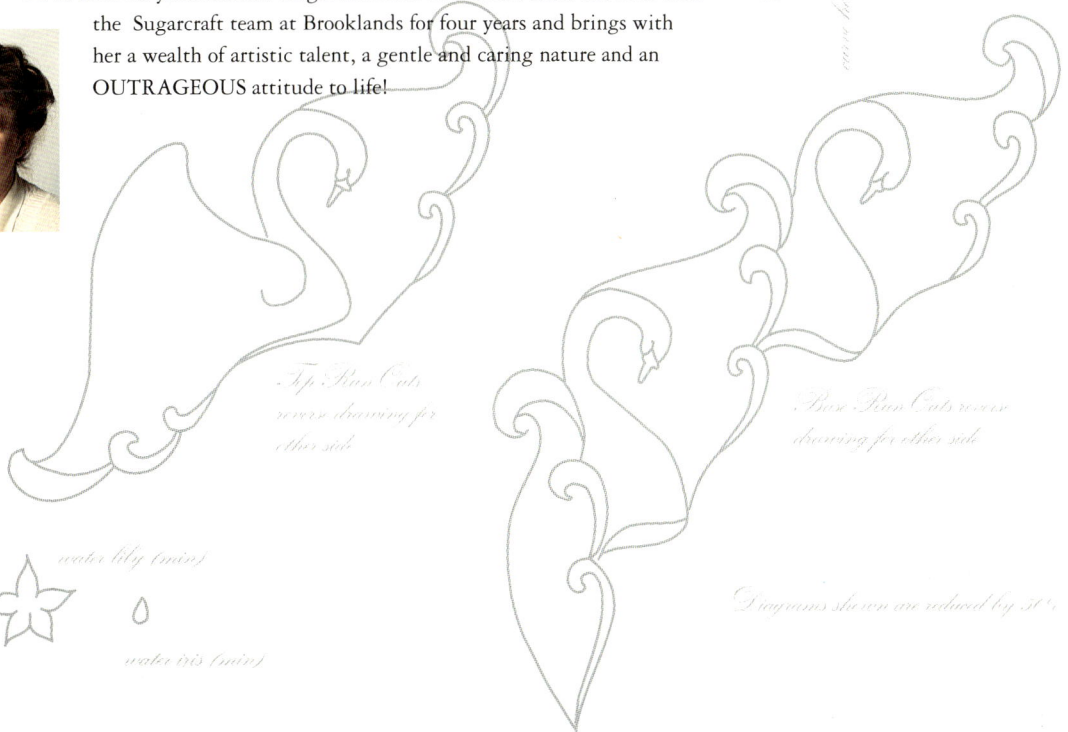

Techniques: Runouts, Marbling 2, Modelling, Pressure piping, Flowers

Orbital Runway

ORBITAL RUNWAY

I watched a Swedish television programme on perpetual motion that had no script and lasted 20 minutes - incredible! I watched it years ago but I have never forgotten it. This is not your average domino run!

Instructions

This cake can be attempted by novice and expert alike. Building the pieces is the easy bit and designing it takes imagination and patience! It is addictive work - see if you can make your own even better and brighter than mine (bet you can't!)

The Jingle Speaker - don't stick the speaker down - you need to reset it! Place a little fence around to stop the speaker tipping over.

Centrepiece - the height of the centrepiece must be in balance with the whole design. Easy! keep adding bits until you feel happy...

Flags - spell out "Happy Birthday"

Windmill - make the hole in the centre large enough to allow the windmill to spin. Make a stopper at each end of the pin to stop the windmill falling off.

Snake Pass - be careful here with the angles or the ball can get stuck half way.

Chez Gawen (lecturer at Brooklands) has a broad knowledge of the food industry covering bakery, confectionery, patisserie, catering, sugarcraft and food technology. She worked in the 'new product development' department at Manor Bakeries - helping a well known gentleman make exceedingly good cakes! Chez brings this wealth of knowledge, a true sense of fun and her ability to 'get things done' to the sugarcraft team at Brooklands.

Parfait of Bitter Chocolate and Almond on a Pear Coulis

PARFAIT OF BITTER CHOCOLATE AND ALMOND ON A PEAR COULIS

Nicola Burroughs has been studying sugarcraft, as a hobby, for nearly four years and has gained the City and Guilds 7900 Creative Studies qualification. Nicola is Junior Sous Chef and Pastry Chef at Wentworth Golf Club and the idea for this parfait came to her whilst planning new menus. Niki says, "It is one of my favourite desserts as the flavouring of the bitter chocolate and the almond blend well together and the marzipan adds that extra dimension of almond taste. The parfait may be presented any way you wish but I find this way particularly attractive. I hope you enjoy making and of course, eating it as much as I do".

Ingredients

8 egg yolks
200g (8oz) Silver Spoon granulated sugar
500ml (20 fl.oz) double cream
150g (6oz) dark bitter chocolate
2 measures amaretto liqueur
50g (2oz) roasted flaked almonds
50g (2oz) cocoa powder
100g (4oz) marzipan
few drops of almond essence
extra chocolate and roasted almonds for decoration
6 large pears
1 measure Poire William liqueur

1. Place sugar in a small pan, barely cover with water and boil until the soft ball stage is reached (119°C)
2. Whisk the yolks until thickened and double in volume. When the sugar is ready, pour on to the whisking yolks and continue whisking until the mixture is cool.
3. Whisk the double cream to a flopping consistency in a separate bowl.
4. Take 1/3rd of the egg mixture out of the bowl and place to one side. Melt the chocolate and pour into the remaining 2/3rds of the egg mixture,still whisking. Add the cocoa powder. Fold in 2/3rds of the whipped cream.
5. To the other 1/3rd of the egg mixture, fold in the remaining whipped cream, add the amaretto and the almonds.
6. Line your terrine mould with silicon paper on the bottom and pour half the chocolate mixture into it. Pipe the almond mixture on to the chocolate mixture, trying to keep a rounded shape. Pour over the remaining chocolate mixture and place into the freezer overnight.
7. Run a warm knife around the sides of the parfait to release from the terrine. Roll out marzipan thinly, on the final roll use a basket weave rolling pin. Turn the marzipan over and place the parfait on it. Wrap around and trim off the excess. With the join at the bottom, blowtorch the top of the marzipan to give a scorched effect. Place the parfait back in the freezer for at least one hour or until you are ready to serve it.
8. Pear Coulis

   Peel and chop the pears and simmer in a saucepan with a tablespoon of water and the Poire William liqueur until soft. Put through a blender,add sugar to taste and refrigerate.
9. To Serve

   Spoon coulis into the middle of a plate. Slice the parfait with a hot knife and place on the coulis. Scatter chocolate curls and roasted almonds around the edge of the plate, finish with dusting of icing sugar and tuille biscuit.

   Chocolate Curls

   Melt dark chocolate and pour on a marble slab, spread with a palette knife until chocolate starts to dry. Hold a large cooks knife at 45° angle on the chocolate, push the knife away to form the curl.

Almond Tuilles
125g (5oz) flour
200g (8 oz) butter
200g (8oz) Silver Spoon caster sugar
150g (6oz) nibbed almonds

Cream the butter and sugar until pale and fluffy, add the flour and almonds. Wrap in cling film. Chill. To cook: roll into little balls on a greased baking tray. Flatten each ball out as much as possible. Bake at 200°C. When pale gold remove from oven, leave to cool slightly, lift off and shape over a rolling pin.

Partridge in a Pear Tree

PARTRIDGE

Although this design is presented on a board, it could easily be made into an unusual cake. However, it may be more acceptable to coat the cake in brown, rather than black marzipan.

Instructions

Take four pieces of yellow marzipan, two walnut size and two marble size and mould to look like pears. Cut each down the middle to make eight halves. Dust or airbrush with food colours and place pears in position on the base. Neaten edges.

Take another piece of marzipan, the size of a tennis ball, coloured yellow with a hint of orange and shape to the fat bird. Cut the wings into the top of the bird and then smooth and round them into shape. Stipple a mixture of brown and orange colouring on to the bird to give it the rust colouring of feathers and beak. The same colour is added to a small piece of marzipan, rolled out and placed on the head of the bird, cut and moulded to make the skull cap. Cut and mould a piece of black marzipan on the birds face and neck. A white face mask is cut from sugarpaste and attached in position. Cut small rounds of white sugarpaste with an icing tube and place on the breast of the bird as spots. The birds' neck ruffle is cut and stuck with egg white.Roll dark brown marzipan into shapes of the tree branches and score them with a fork to create texture. Cut some green marzipan for leaves, mark veins, spray with extra colour and attach to branches.

Susan Beams was born in England, lived in Africa for 20 years and on returning to England met her husband. She started decorating cakes for her children's birthdays. As a housekeeper in a school and a seamstress, she still finds time to study the 7900 Creative Studies course at Brooklands.

Pumpkin

PUMPKIN

Cake - 2 round sponges sandwiched with buttercream. Carve the grooves with a sharp knife. Place the surplus sponge on top with buttercream. Mask the whole of the pumpkin with buttercream. Roll out lilac sugarpaste and lay over the front third of the pumpkin. Leave to crust over. Roll out orange sugarpaste and wrap over the pumpkin. It can be done in two separate halves. Smooth down well. Cut out windows and doors. Leave to set. Windows and doors are made of green pastillage. The decorations on these are made of sugarpaste. Stalk - green tapered sausage of pastillage and squeeze grooves with tweezers. Petal dust the pumpkin and stalk with various shades of orange and green. Chimney - Made from pastillage, base is a sausage, then three graduated circles, top is a cone. Mark bricks with a knife, petal dust.

Mouse (basic figure)

Teeth - these must be made up and dry before you start your figures. Roll out a rectangle of white flowerpaste and cut out teeth. **Body** - white marzipan, rolled to a cone shape. Flatten the top. **Head** - A cone, indent with a ball tool to make the eye sockets. (Press the ball tool in firmly and then move the handle upwards). Dampen finger and thumb, stroke up top of head, snip with scissors to create tuft of hair. Small ball of pink marzipan for the nose. Whilst face is still soft insert cut stamens for whiskers and push teeth in at an angle. **Ears** - 2 white balls and 2 tiny pink balls of marzipan. Press your finger into the white balls, leaving a thick edge. Press a pink ball into each ear and smooth. While the face is still soft attach the ears and press in the teeth. **Arms** - white marzipan sausage tapered at both ends. Cut in centre. Wide end is cuff, make a hole in end for hand. **Hands** - white marzipan cone shape and flatten the end. Cut out triangle for the thumb and two cuts for the fingers. Insert into the cuffs. **Eyes** - Pipe with white royal icing No.2 tube and brown No.1 tube. Pipe pupils off centre to give character. Leave overnight to set.Paint brows and lashes with 000 brush and brown colouring. **Tails** - brown marzipan tapered sausage. Attach to 'back end' of body.

Dressed Mice

Trousers - sausage of marzipan cut down the centre. **Skirt** - cone of marzipan for body. Make garrett frill from sugarpaste, frill. Dampen marzipan body and wrap frill around the base of the cone, spiralling up to the waist. Small cone of marzipan for the body. Make arms of sugarpaste and hands of marzipan. Belts from sugarpaste, needles from pastillage and the knitting is royal icing. **Guitar** - thick yellow flowerpaste, cut an oak leaf, vein. Cut out a circle near top of the leaf. Strings are made from stamens which are anchored down with tiny strips of paste.

Moss - green sugarpaste textured with nylon washing up brush.

Pram - hollow out a light brown ball of flowerpaste. Indent the outside with a ball tool to represent a walnut. Roll out the flowerpaste and cut out and mark four circles for wheels. Leave to dry. When dry, stick wheels on pram with 'glue'. Cut out strip for handle and bend to shape. Leave to dry. When dry attach to pram with 'glue'. Pillow and quilt made of sugarpaste. When dry paint as required.

Pat Ashby has been teaching sugarcraft for over 23 years and is the author of several books on the subject. Pat has travelled across the globe demonstrating her art and has appeared on TV and radio. Her talents are not restricted to sugarcraft,to which she always brings light-hearted excellence, since she is also a qualified ASA and STA swimming instructor, specialising in teaching the disabled.

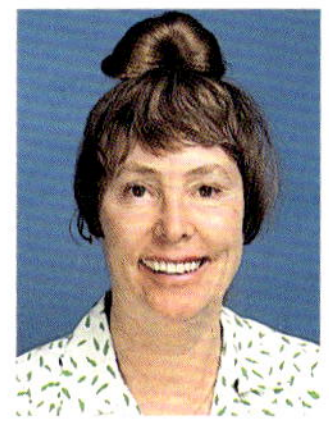

Roman Frieze

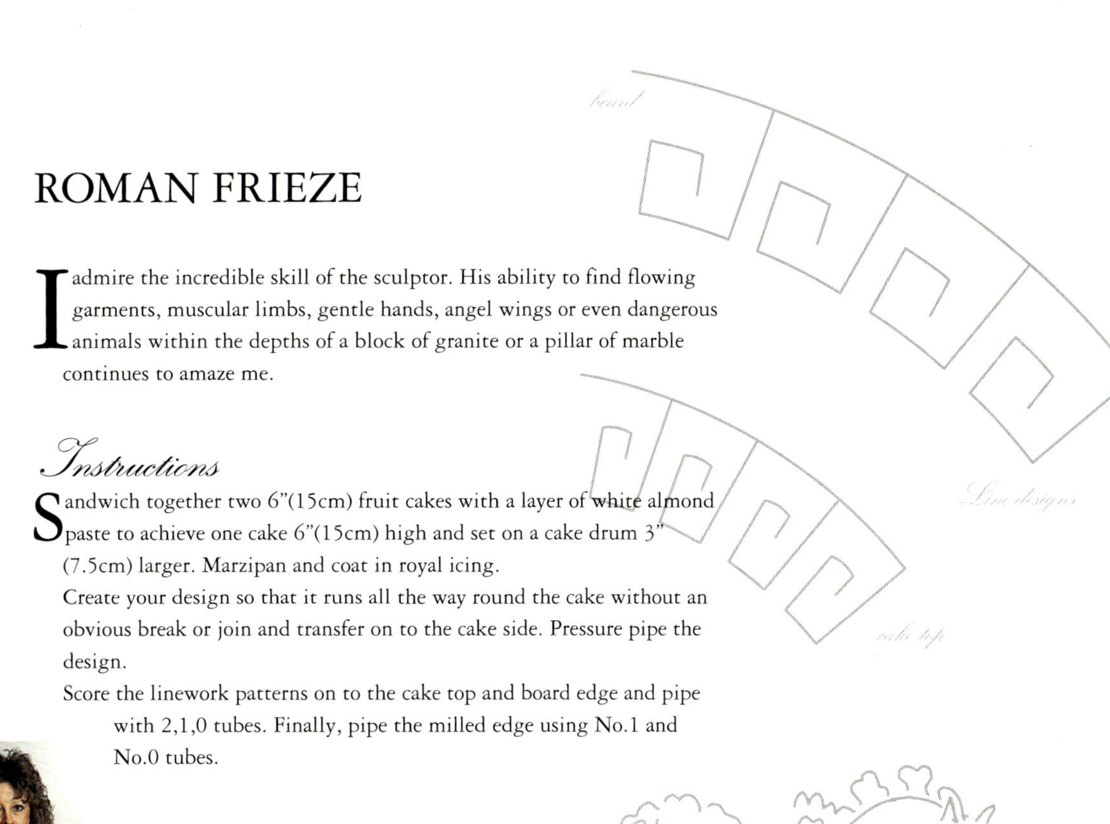

ROMAN FRIEZE

I admire the incredible skill of the sculptor. His ability to find flowing garments, muscular limbs, gentle hands, angel wings or even dangerous animals within the depths of a block of granite or a pillar of marble continues to amaze me.

Instructions

Sandwich together two 6"(15cm) fruit cakes with a layer of white almond paste to achieve one cake 6"(15cm) high and set on a cake drum 3" (7.5cm) larger. Marzipan and coat in royal icing.

Create your design so that it runs all the way round the cake without an obvious break or join and transfer on to the cake side. Pressure pipe the design.

Score the linework patterns on to the cake top and board edge and pipe with 2,1,0 tubes. Finally, pipe the milled edge using No.1 and No.0 tubes.

Jackie Kuflik

Techniques: Pressure piping.

SAILING

One of my favourite places is Hengistbury Head in Bournemouth. It has the sea on one shore and the harbour on the other. As I write this my children are flying their kites there and they will probably scramble up the headland to look out to the Isle of Wight.

There is no pattern for this cake. It is here to encourage you to take a white cake and make it your canvas, to mix up a dozen bags of different coloured royal icing and make them your pencils and to use your imagination and your memory as your subject to paint. This record of my favourite place took six hours to complete and has survived a number of car journeys.

Sugar is a remarkable substance. What you believe to be very fragile turns out to have great strength. Chris and I continue to surprise ourselves with what is possible with this medium. Patience, practice, imagination - enjoy!

Jackie Kuflik

Sailing

Techniques: Bridgeless extension work and pinwork

BAHRAIN

Out of the blue and 10 days notice, Chris and I are planning and designing a 12 foot high wedding cake for 3,000 - in sponge, 10 tiers, marbled and hand painted, and decorated in sugar flowers - in Bahrain. Ten days later we are on a Gulf Air night flight surrounded by boxes of sugar flowers (they took three seats on their own) a kit box and a pallet full of ingredients and equipment in the hold below our feet. We arrived at the Inter-Continental hotel where we were shown our room and two hours later, the pastry kitchen.

Ian Ashmore, pastry chef, soon realised that the next week of his life was going to be different, not only was he going to be making a cake for a Royal Wedding but so were these two ... from England. We worked a minimum of 15 hours a day for the next six days, often having to finish to get out of the way of the night baker. We became the novelty act in the kitchens of this very large hotel as our cake grew before their eyes.

The wedding is held in an enormous marquee on the Emir's estates. The normal inhabitants don't go there so our first lorry driver got lost, trouble was, Chris was with him and she didn't know where to go either.

At 7 the next morning we had to be away to the wedding to decorate the cake that Ian was constructing (and was still constructing and had been doing so for the past 24 hours) Ian was making a palm tree - 14 feet high - with a climbing snake of cake all the way to the top. The scaffolding was shaky but you get used to heights, don't you?

The wedding was a truly amazing event - three nights of dancing, eating and socialising in wonderful surroundings for a most charming and beautiful bride.

Chris Jeffcoate & Jackie Kuflik

Sunflowers

SUNFLOWERS

Last year we were asked to come up with an idea that we hoped would suggest summer, be fairly spectacular and simple to create in a short time. The design relies on vibrant colours and large detail to turn an average sized cake into something joyous. The sunflowers made us smile - we hope they make you smile too.

Instructions

Marzipan and coat in sugarpaste a 10" cake on a 12" board. Using templates provided cut flower heads from pastillage and score each petal along its length with a cocktail stick to produce veining. Soften edges of petals with fingertips and dry over an upturned savarin mould with a circle of card in the centre to avoid the shape falling too deep. Support some petals with cotton wool to create more movement. Repeat with a second flower head of the same size placing on top of the first flower and leave to dry. Make three flowers in all. Glue each pair of flower heads together with royal icing. To make the domed centre, make a doughnut of marzipan, 3" diameter (outside measurement) and 0.5" deep. Roll out pastillage thinly and lay into the well of the doughnut. Trim off excess and leave to dry. When dry, fix centre to petal heads with royal icing. Colour as required with airbrush or painting techniques. Make the leaves in various sizes with thin pastillage and leave to dry (6-7 leaves required) in natural shapes and not completely flat.

To assemble the cake, glue two of the flowerheads to the side of the cake with royal icing. Push the leaves into the sugarpaste covering of the cake. Fix the final flowerhead to a length of dowel or plastic rod using royal icing. Cover the visible dowel with green floristry tape and insert into the cake. Finish by tying a length of paper ribbon around the bottom of the cake.

Max and Greg have been creating their special kind of cake artistry for five years. Never formally trained, their first commission was a cake for Max's mum. From that first step they have gone on to make cakes for pop stars and royalty. They appear on television and have written two successful books.

Diagrams shown are reduced to 50%

Teddy Bears

TEDDY BEARS

I was inspired to make these by a friend who had seen my teddy bears made out of salt dough and suggested I reproduce them in an edible form as a fun gift idea for children or an amusing cake decoration. Marzipan is the ideal medium.

Instructions

Body - 1.5 oz (40g) piece of white marzipan, shape into a ball. Flatten gently with the palm of hand or a small non-stick rolling pin to produce a rounded shape approximately 0.25" (1cm) thick.

Head - shape a smaller ball in the same way and gently press into the top of the body using a little egg white to join. Make a smaller ball for the snout and flatten on one side by pressing the ball on a work surface. Attach to head with egg white and add a tiny red ball of marzipan to the snout for the nose.

Trousers - roll out a thin square of coloured marzipan and cut a semi-circle shape at the top. Place over the body just above waist level and trim bottom half to teddy shape. Neatly tuck the cut edge under the body. For the braces cut a thin strip from rolled out marzipan, divide in two and position.

Paws & Ears - roll out a finger-sized sausage of white marzipan and cut six small pieces of equal size. Roll each piece into a ball and flatten a little. Moisten with egg white and position four on the body and two on the head. Indent centre of ears and paint brown. Paint teddy's mouth with the same colour. Paint tongue in red.

Pipe eyes and buttons on trousers with No.1 tube and white royal icing. When dry, paint in black pupils on eyes and threads on buttons in black. Other items can be created with marzipan that has been cut or modelled and further detail added in piped royal icing, e.g. baby, football, candy cane, parcels, kite, book, flowers.

Catherine Pearson has been studying sugarcraft for three years, two of which at Brooklands College where she is currently following the 7900 Creative Studies Course. She became interested in sugarcraft as an extension of her hobby of modelling in salt dough.

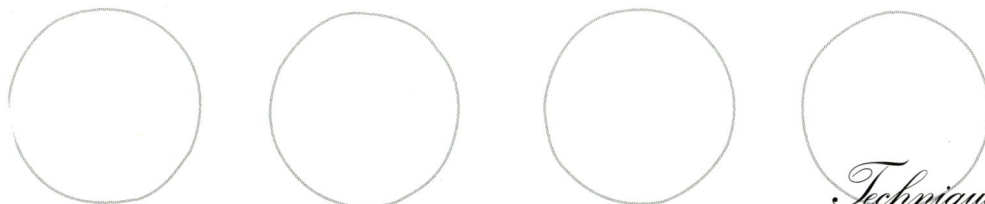

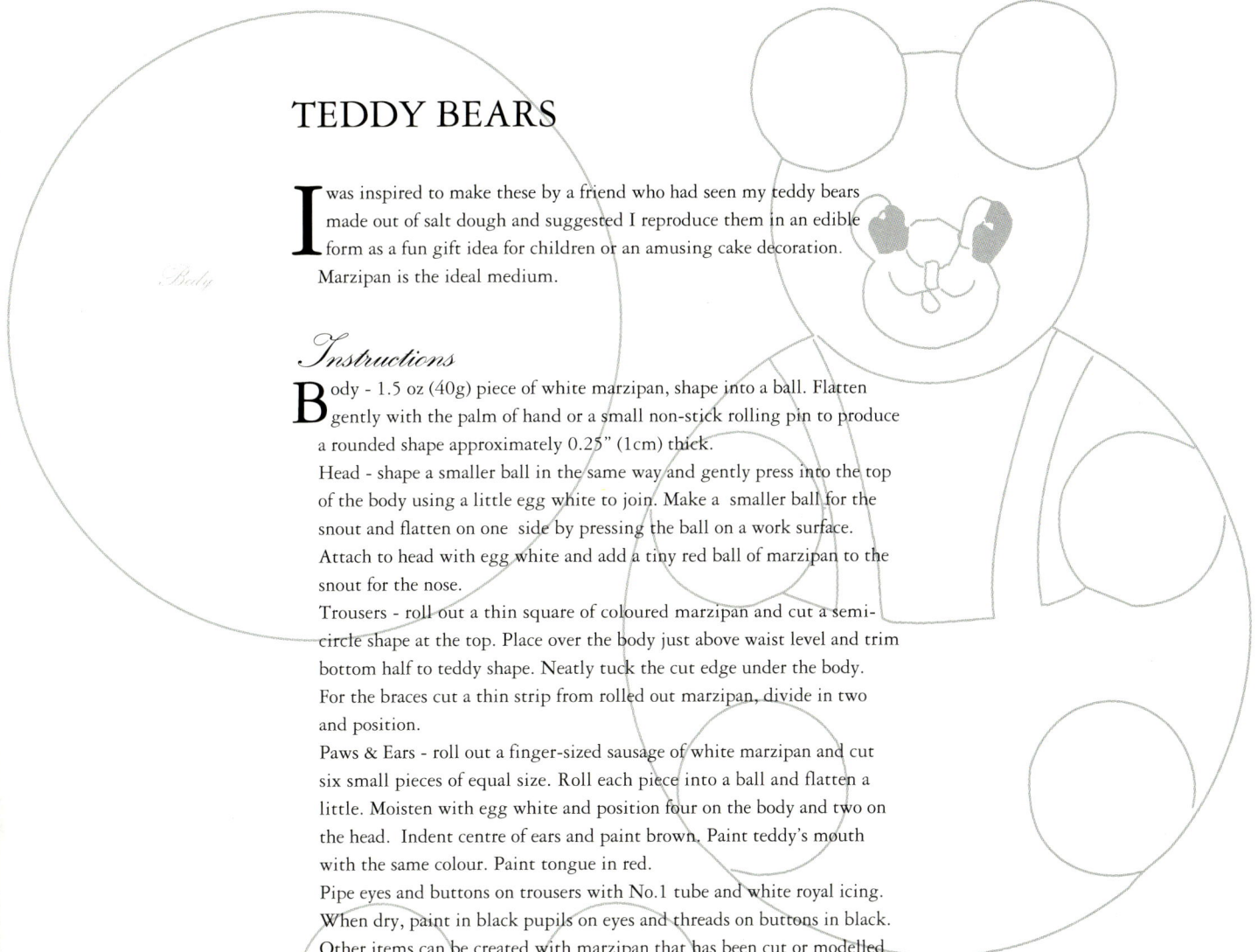

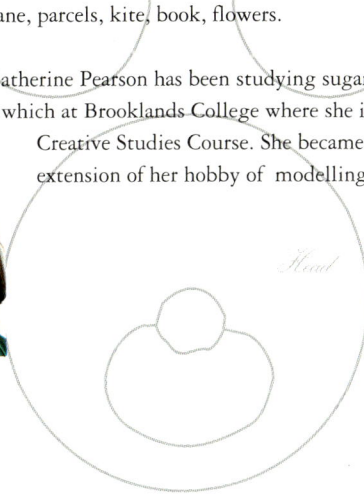

Water

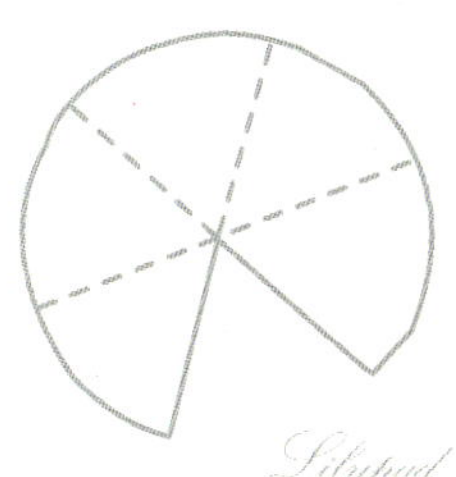

WATER

The idea for the shape of the cake came from a chair design by Mary Little and the water influence from a Wedgwood plate dated 1806 which had a stylised Waterlily pattern. The extension work design also came from a piece of Wedgwood in the shape of a shell but now it is completed makes me think of waves.

Instructions

The three tiers of this cake can be cut from a 14" (35cm) round fruit cake - giving a 10" (25cm) round for the base. The remaining crescent is cut into two pieces, one piece larger than the other. The points of the crescent will need trimming.

Marzipan and sugarpaste the cakes and boards. Mark the sides of the cakes in preparation for the extension work which has a 1" repeat pattern.

Mark each section onto the cake with a pin prick 1" up from the base board. Pipe a bulb of coloured icing over the pin hole, then pipe another bulb on top of the first one. When dry pipe the extension work with a No.0 tube, as diagram. Airbrush or dust the centre of the round cake with blue colour to represent water.

The water lilies and lily pads are fixed to the cake with egg white or gum arabic glue whilst the irises and bulrushes are put into posy picks.

Arrange small 'stones' of paste around but not covering the holes made by the posy picks.

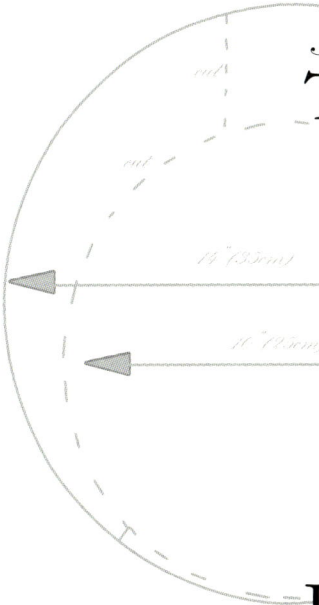

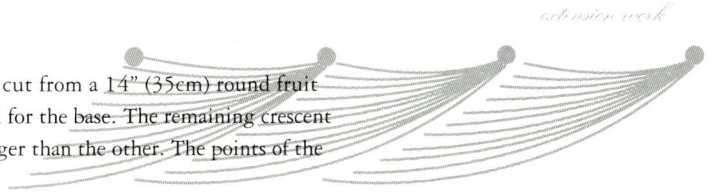

Linda Jefferson trained at Westminster Technical College as a home economist and started teaching food studies and cake decorating in 1977, furthering her studies at Hendon and Cassio and most recently at Brooklands. Currently Linda is teaching City and Guilds 121 at Hendon and City and Guilds 7900 at Weald College, an external verifier for City and Guilds, a provisional judge for the British Sugarcraft Guild and is studying City and Guilds 7900 Creative Studies, Part II at Brooklands.

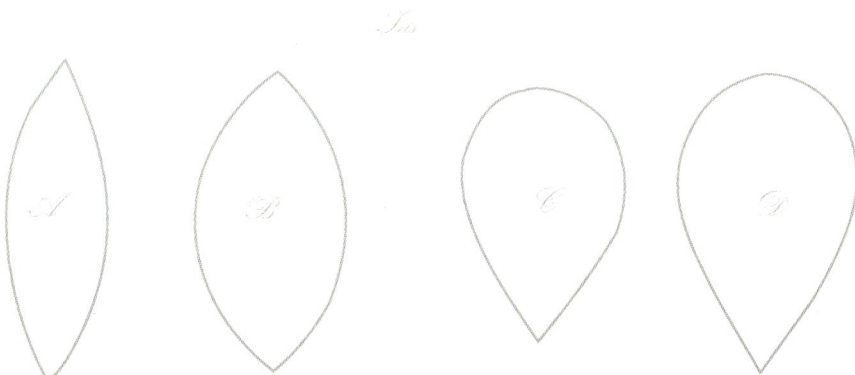

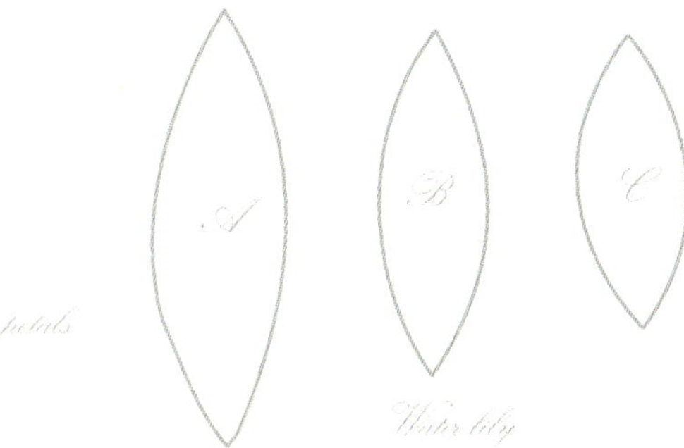

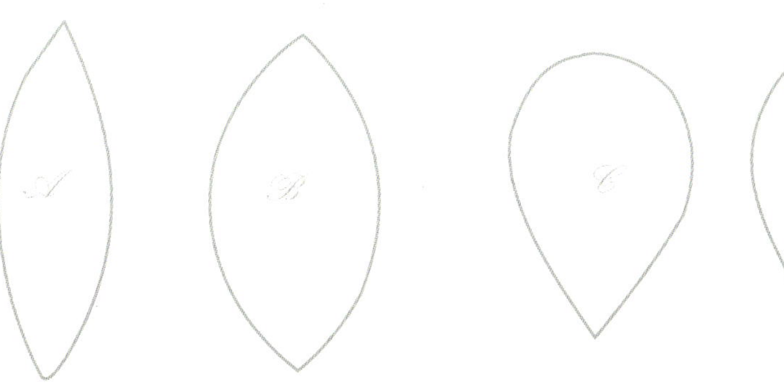

Techniques: Extension work, Flowers

Wisteria

WISTERIA

Ideas for retirement cakes are few and as I enjoy working in fine detail I designed this intricate little cottage. I couldn't find Wisteria instructions in any books so enlisted the help of Wisley, from whom I received detailed drawings and descriptions. I was amazed to discover that the leaves grow on a different stem to the flowers and there are always nine leaves to each stem.

Instructions

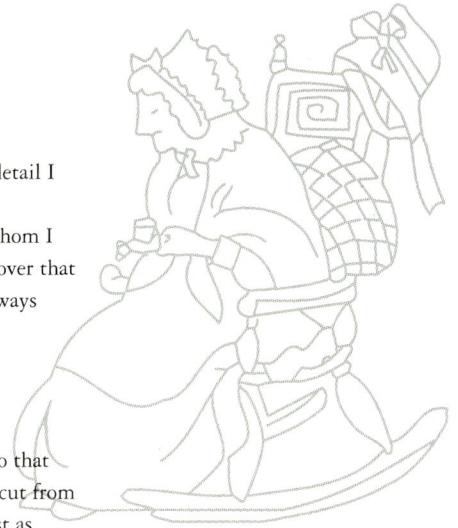

Cut an oval cake in half but at an angle and slide the two halves so that they are offset. Coat in marzipan and sugarpaste. The cottage is cut from sugarpaste of various thicknesses, pieces 2 and 4 being the thickest as they are in the foreground.

Assemble the basic shapes, like pieces of a jigsaw, on to the cake and when set add colour and detail with a variety of mediums, such as royal icing, marzipan, flowerpaste, etc.

Transfer the side design to the cake and pressure pipe using a selection of coloured royal icing. Alternatively, make a runout motif on waxed paper fixed to an oval cake tin and glue to the side of the cake when dry.

Make and arrange the Wisteria in flower picks at the two ends of the cake, trailing the flowers down to the board.

Peter Reed has spent his working life in catering, from ocean liners to his present job with Frimley Park Hospital Trust as Food Production Manager. Sugarcraft is a recent hobby and he is now training at Brooklands.

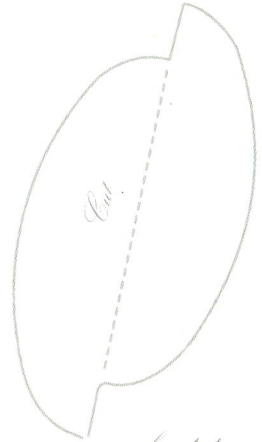

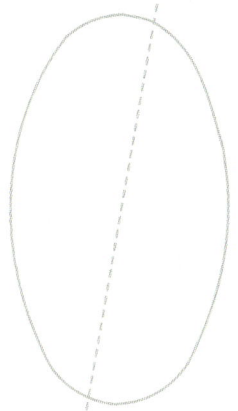

Techniques: Relief work 1, Runouts, Pressure piping, Flowers

Yin and Yang

YIN AND YANG

The idea for this cake came from China, using flowers and colours from their festivals and the Yin and Yang symbol.

Instructions

Cut the cakes from a 12" round fruit cake using the diagram as a guide. Marzipan and sugarpaste the cakes and boards and leave to dry.

Pipe the stringwork orchid on to the sides of the cake in the order shown tilting the cake where necessary to encourage the loops to fall in the right direction. Pipe dots on the points of the design to lift each loop away from the next. Lines 1,2,7 & 8 were piped with the cake the right way up, lines 3,4,5 & 6 with the cake upside down.

Stringwork - use the patterns given to make templates for the sides of the cakes and mark the points on to the cake surface. Drop loops from these points with No.1 tube and finish with embroidery and graduated dots.

Make and arrange the flowers on the cakes.

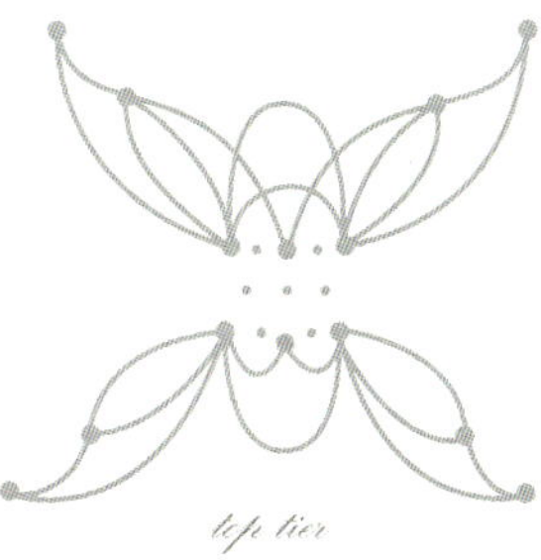

Jayne Smith has been involved with sugarcraft for 10 years since a visit, whilst training to be a cook, to Hotelympia. She attended Adult Education classes, gained certificates in cake decorating and design and now teaches the subject. Jane is currently studying Part II at Brooklands.

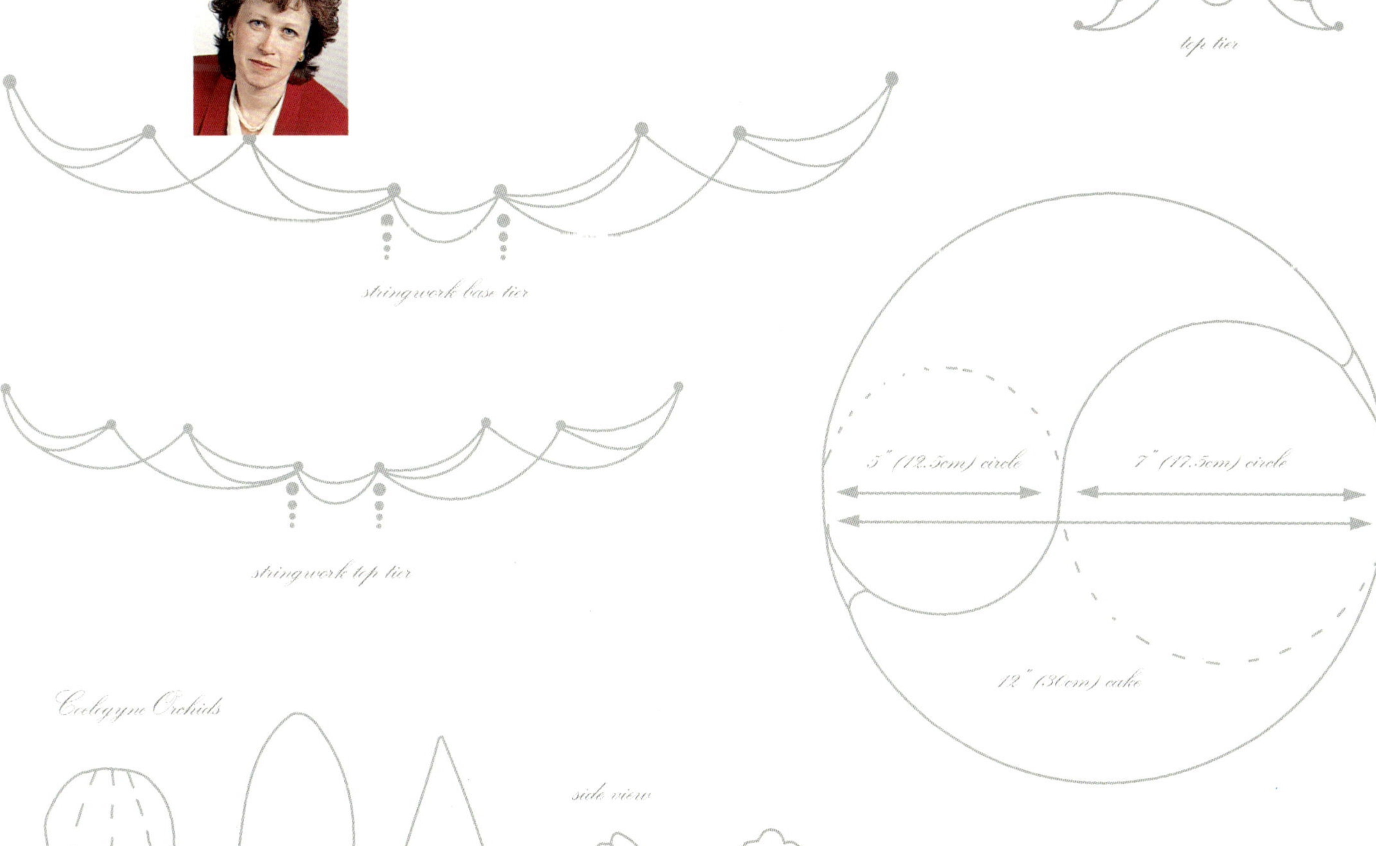

A B C

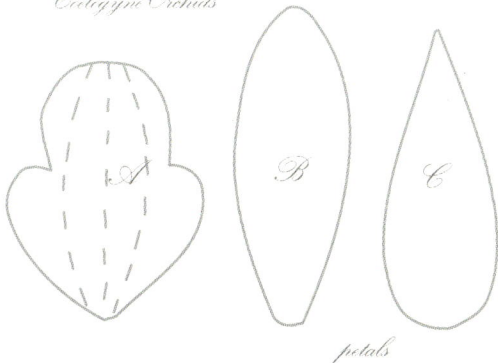

petals

side view

view from below

columns

TECHNIQUES

Beyond the usual recommendations and instructions outlined in so many sugarcraft books we have given in this section our own recommendations for success. Some of the techniques are new and we hope you will enjoy developing them even further.

Royal Icing - coating

Royal Icing, when first made, is firm and evenly aerated. To achieve good results with coating, the royal icing should be softened (to a soft peak) by adding water. Successful smooth coating can be achieved by applying many thin coats of royal icing over a period of time. For competition work and particularly when using dummy cakes, a matured icing will give excellent results.

This can be achieved over a period of weeks, coating one cake from a single bowl or mix of royal icing which has been covered with a damp cloth and plastic bag. This allows the royal icing to absorb some of the dampness from the cloth every time it is covered, thereby thinning the sugar between applications. The royal icing should be stirred carefully each time before use by hand only so that no air is introduced into the mixture. The final coating should be a thin skim of royal icing which by now should be the consistency of single cream. A good gloss can be obtained by drying this coat under a lamp.

Bridgeless Extension work

(to include stringwork and pinwork)

All the extension work in this book is 'bridgeless' and therefore quite advanced. We suggest that you try bridged extension work before trying this technique. Instructions are available in many sugarcraft books.
Stability is the key to all bridgeless extension work. This is achieved by piping the main support lines in contact with the cake at regular intervals.
Unusual shapes can be created by the strategic use of oiled pins (vegetable oil) and piping the lines/loops from the cake, over the pins and back to the cake. This can be made even more interesting by tilting the cake to various angles. In all cases, allow each piped line to dry thoroughly before changing the position of the cake.

Care must be taken when piping secondary lines on to main support lines by ensuring that you stop piping underneath the support line. If you touch the support line with the tube it is very likely to break. The use of different lines of colour can create further interesting effects. When trying out these techniques,
PRACTICE WILL CERTAINLY MAKE PERFECT!
CAUTION. Pins can be easily sterilised by immersing in alcohol or boiling water and air-dried before use. Always make sure pins are removed from the cake and the holes they make in the coating are sealed with a small dot of Royal icing immediately.

Lacework

Always use freshly-made royal icing using pure albumen. We prefer to use wax coated tissue paper which releases the very fine pieces of lace quite readily. Pipe the lace pieces with a soft peak icing in a small greaseproof bag using a maximum No. 0 tube. Always pipe the lines towards you, not crossing any lines already piped, which could affect the strength of the overall piece. Remove the lace pieces from the wax tissue when they are well dried, by flexing the tissue and gently easing your thumb underneath each piece.

Very difficult to handle lace pieces can be picked up by using a soft brush (open the bristles of the brush by stabbing on to a hard surface, this allows each lace piece to nestle into the open bristles and allows you to present the piece to the cake.) Apply using a dot or two of soft royal icing either to the surface of the cake or the back of each lace piece.

Embroidery

Always keep embroidery designs simple and easy to copy freehand. Complicated designs that need to be pencilled on are always difficult to cover up and you will often get black marks. If you have to transfer the design it is better to prick or scratch it on with a pin. Use a soft peak royal icing with a maximum No. 0 tube in a small greaseproof bag.

Brush Embroidery

There are different methods of transferring the design on to the cake surface. If your design is simple then you may be able to transfer the design by piping freehand. If transferring on to sugarpaste you can use the impression method. Firstly, place a sheet of perspex over your design and with a No.1 tube and firm royal icing copy the design on to the perspex sheet. Allow to dry well. Coat the cake with the sugarpaste and whilst the coating is still soft press the piped design into position required (ensuring the surface of the sugarpaste is not sticky).

Remember, the transferred design will be in reverse to the way you have piped it on to the perspex, and if this is not what you require, reverse the original design first.

For royal iced surfaces, firstly ensure the icing is completely dry and firm. Copy your design by tracing on to the surface of the icing using a sharp, hard graphite pencil (3H or 4H is ideal as a HB pencil is too soft and will smudge). Alternatively, scratch the design on with a pin.

A soft consistency, well beaten royal icing is ideal for this technique. Apply the royal icing from a small bag, with or without tubes. A damp paintbrush, of a size suitable to the piece of work, e.g. No.2 or No.3, is used to brush the surface of the icing from the outside towards the centre of each shape. Always work from the back of the design towards the front. To give depth to your work, extra sugar will be required for the areas which stand out or are closer to the foreground. When using the graphite pencil transfer method always be sure to pipe the icing a tubes width BEHIND the pencil line brushing forward to cover the line completely.

Pressure Piping

Of course, the majority of royal icing techniques are applied with some degree of pressure but we are looking here at a technique that has varying degrees of pressure to obtain a specific effect.

Firstly, use royal icing, freshly made with pure albumen, as for runouts. The consistency of the royal icing will vary depending upon the effects required, from soft peak to the consistency required for curved runouts. We stress that experimentation is vital for this technique, however, we hope that these few guidelines will help.

To obtain a smooth surface, keep the icing moving by 'scribbling' closely as if you were colouring in with pencils.

To create height use a firm icing and after creating a smooth surface force the royal icing from underneath to create bulk. The use of a damp paintbrush will help but care should be taken not to make the surface too wet. When removing the tube from the surface of the icing, always remove from the side, never from the top.

Use small greaseproof bags, with or without tubes, and a variety of sizes of paintbrushes which should be of a very good quality.

Scoring

The surface of a royal iced cake is usually expected to be smooth yet here is just one way of producing a texture in royal icing which gives a new and exciting effect.When the royal iced cake is perfectly dry and firm score lines into the surface at regular intervals, using a scalpel and icing ruler.

The depth of lines and the ease of scoring them in, can be changed depending upon the pressure used and whether the royal icing contains glycerin or not. This texture can be accentuated by colouring with airbrushing or powders.

Run Out Work

The secret to quality run outs is to use royal icing made with pure albumen. When making the royal icing, never overbeat as your aim is to have as little air in the mixture as possible. It is also important to select a suitable non stick surface to make your runouts on, e.g. waxed paper, cling film, polythene, or purpose made sheets now available.

Motifs - there are various ways of producing small pictures as motifs, by outlining first with a fine tube in either brown or coloured royal icing (at standard consistency) and filling in with softened royal icing, the consistency of single cream OR by not outlining at all but using a slightly firmer royal icing to fill in the various shapes and areas of each picture. Understanding your various consistencies of royal icing will take experimentation and practice to get it right.

Collars - in general these are outlined first as above (motifs) and filled in with soft royal icing. Care must be taken not to overfill the shapes, particularly those with apertures or narrow angles, as the sugar will try to flow together. When flooding a full collar or large areas, flood a small section at a time, going from one side to the other. If it were a clock face, flood 12, then 11, then 1, then 10, and so on, so that the sugar does not have time to crust.

To remove air bubbles when making the runout always use a bag with a small hole cut. Any bubbles that are created when flooding can be removed by pricking with a cocktail stick or fine paintbrush.

To obtain a good gloss for your runouts always place them under a warm lamp immediately to crust over. Only leave under the lamp for about 15 minutes and as soon as a crust is formed remove the lamp and then place your runout in a warm dry atmosphere to complete the drying process.

We remove our runouts by sliding a feeler gauge between the non stick surface and the underside of the runout. (feeler gauges, used for measuring the gap in sparkplugs, can be purchased from car maintenance type shops). Attaching the runouts to the cake surface can be quite a nerve racking experience. We have found that the best way is to be BRAVE and POSITIVE with every movement. Stick the runout with soft royal icing and once the runout is in position do not press down but allow the runout to settle itself using its own weight.

Runouts - curved. Curved formers can be made by using thin, firm cardboard, shaped over the edge of a straight edged knife. Once the correct shape has been achieved you will need to secure the card shape on to a strong board with sticky tape. Cover the formers with waxed tissue and seal in place with dots of royal icing or masking tape for easy removal. Follow the guidelines above for making the runouts but note that the royal icing in this instance should be slightly firmer. To test that the icing is the correct consistency pipe two large bulbs of the icing one on top of the other when they should hold their shape but if the surface of the icing is moved they should blend into one another. Do make plenty of spares to allow for breakages. Remove curved runouts from the waxed tissue by turning upside down on to a soft surface, e.g. sponge or tea towel, gently ease opposite ends of the paper towards each other, lifting at the same time, to release the paper from the back of the runout. As above, use soft icing to apply the runout to the cake.

Snow

Take some royal icing with glycerin and put in a greaseproof bag. Leave to harden for a couple of days. Remove the paper and grate on a cheese grater. Attach to surfaces with a fine mist of water sprayed on the receiving surface. This gives a coarser effect than icing sugar.

Sugarpaste - coating

Always use a light dusting of icing sugar on your board or table when rolling out sugarpaste. Dusting the top surface of the sugarpaste to prevent sticking should be avoided where at all possible as this dries the paste prematurely and will also give a dull or matte finish.

As soon as the paste is rolled to the required size apply to the cake without delay being careful not to trap any pockets of air. If you are dealing with complicated shaped cakes, smoothing the sugarpaste on will take some time, so to prevent cracking rub a small knob of white vegetable fat into the palms of your hands and continue stretching and smoothing the paste to fit. Trim as required.

Relief Work

There are many different types and techniques of relief work,under a variety of guises, which use sugarpaste, marzipan, etc.

Relief Work 1.

Layers of pastes in various thicknesses are cut out and blocked together like pieces of a jigsaw directly on to the required surface. Thick paste is used for areas in the foreground whilst thin paste is required for background areas. This technique is ideal for pictures that require little depth or have many intricate details.

Relief Work 2.

This gives greater depth, sometimes called 'half-relief' when each shape is virtually half the depth of the original shape, e.g. a pear would be moulded and cut in half before laying into position. Reshaping will probably be necessary as you will distort the shape when cutting. Larger areas are best modelled to the basic shape, placed over the template and the underside flattened. The top surface should then be rounded towards the edges to give the appearance of a continuing smooth shape. Marzipan or sugarpaste are ideal for this technique.

Relief Work 3.

This technique uses the cake, which has been cut to the required outline shape, to give initial depth. Further depth is added at the marzipan stage. Cut the template into main sections to assist you in cutting out the marzipan and apply it to the cake in required depths (using boiled jam) similar to technique 1. above. Colour sugarpaste as required and apply in sections but of the same thickness throughout, smoothing the joins and sculpting where necessary with fingertips and modelling tools. Further colour and textures are then added to complete your design.

Relief Work 4.

This method creates a very fine finish using flowerpaste as the main material. Having chosen the design, make a basic support shape from sugarpaste and place in position, creating the start of height and depth of the finished piece on which you build the layers of flowerpaste in finer detail. If you are creating fabrics, always cut the flowerpaste larger to allow for tucking, pleating and folding as required. Use modelling tools to give detail for features and finish the work with any extra painting depending upon the effect you want to achieve.

Sculpturing

This is the technique of using the cake and the way it is cut to create shape, depth, perspective, etc and is often used to best effect when making novelty cakes. You should use a firm sponge (see recipe) and a sharp knife to create layers of cake for height and sculpture or carve for definition. Always use templates to help as planning is very important to ensure that you do not waste cake unnecessarily. Do not overfill your cakes with buttercream or jam when making sculptured designs as they will become unstable. If necessary use boiled jam or chill the buttercreamed cake well before coating.

Modelling

Three dimensional form can be created in marzipan, sugarpaste and flowerpaste (and its derivatives)

Marzipan - always use at room temperature. A good firm modelling paste (see recipe) is most suitable. Always start by shaping the paste into a ball to remove creases or cracks before continuing to form basic shapes. Model to finer detail by using fingers or modelling tools, gently easing into the shapes required and never forcing and thereby cracking the surface. When modelling with your hands always use the pads of your fingers in a tapping motion and not the tips which will give fingermarks. If the marzipan gets sticky to the touch keep your fingers moist by using a damp cloth. If necessary use gum arabic or melted chocolate to glue pieces together - royal icing is unsuitable.

Sugarpaste - this is naturally softer in texture than modelling marzipan and so cannot be used for larger, unsupported pieces. The modelling techniques are the same as marzipan above, however, if the paste gets sticky use cornflour or icing sugar AND NOT DAMPNESS to make handling easier. Glue together with gum arabic or royal icing. Alternatively, soften some sugarpaste with egg white to make a 'slip' (as used in pottery) as a glue. This can be piped or brushed into place.

Flowerpaste - gives a firmer finish than sugarpaste. Techniques for sugarpaste (above) apply for this medium but remember that as flowerpaste is firmer it allows for finer details and works well in miniature. Make the glue (or 'slip') from flowerpaste and egg white.

Pastillage Work

Pastillage (Gum Paste) - there are many recipes (and names) for this type of sugar, our favourite recipe gives a smooth, fine finish which will always dry hard (like porcelain). This paste is used for rolling out and cutting shapes, which when dry are glued together to create three dimensional form. The 'glue' we recommend is royal icing with a pinch of gum tragacanth added to make a firmer set. The surface of pastillage dries very quickly and you must therefore work quickly to stop it wrinkling or creasing. We always use templates made of card and plan our cutting carefully to prevent panic and wastage. When rolling out, a non stick board is helpful but pastillage is still likely to stick and a fine dusting of cornflour through a muslin bag is our recommended method.

Quickly transfer the rolled out paste to the lightly cornfloured surface on which you are going to dry it before cutting. (Shapes transferred after cutting can easily distort and make assembly difficult if not impossible!)

Cutting - use a long French cook's knife in a rocking motion (from tip to base) for long straight lines and a pizza wheel for curves. Craft knives, scalpels or small pointed knives are best used for small areas or fine detail. Try not to drag your cutting tool through the paste as this will distort the finished item. Drying of the cut shapes can take a few hours to a few days depending upon the size and thickness of the paste. The shapes should be turned regularly to allow for even drying. Large shapes should not be turned too soon (test pieces can be made to give you a guideline as to how the paste is progressing in its drying state).

Cut flat pieces can also be shaped by drying over curved surfaces, i.e. rolling pins, or supported with cotton wool until dry.

Pastillage can also be pressed into preformed moulds which have been dusted with cornflour.

Painting/Airbrushing

Sugar surfaces can be painted with either liquid, paste or powder colours depending upon the effect required. As all sugar is hygroscopic (absorbs water readily) it is advisable to use your brush with as little liquid as possible. Liquid colours can be thinned or diluted with water, paste or powder colours with alcohol (gin, vodka, etc.) to make the colours paler.

When painting do remember to study what you are trying to reproduce. Look for the nuances or style of the piece, the highlights or shaded areas, the variety of shades and tints of any one colour, all of which will help your painting come alive. Take particular care when painting fine detail, especially with faces (portraits) - use very small brushes, delicate colouring and suggestion of lips or eyes. Understate rather than overstate being your watchword. Many paintings have been ruined by poorly painted features (i.e. putting in all the eyelashes or bright pink lips).

Oil painting effects can be achieved by using coloured royal icing or buttercream and applying to the cake surface with artists' palette knives. Many exciting textures can be created using this method. We suggest you practice, developing your own style, before transferring your final plan to your finished cake.

Airbrushing - a technique which is becoming more popular. There are many airbrushes on the market, buy one suited to your pocket.Again, practice is required to achieve good results. Liquid food colours are needed to give even spray. The airbrushing techniques used in this book were aided by the use of stencils.

Marbling

To create the effect of marble on a cake depends on the type of sugar used.

Marbling 1. Sugarpaste marbling is achieved by only half mixing the colour (liquid or paste) into the paste and then rolling out.

Marbling 2. Use a number of solid coloured pastes and blend them together before rolling out.

Marbling 3. Marbling in royal icing is achieved by using soft runout icing and lightly blending together with a cocktail stick or brush. This method is best suited to pre-fabricated runouts.

Marbling 4. Coat the cake in royal icing and allow to dry thoroughly before applying icing whitener, diluted with water, in sweeping motions. The whitener can be coloured as required and should be the consistency of thin cream. It should be applied to the cake as lightly as possible and we recommend using a new nylon pan scourer for this. "Rag-rolling" and "sponging" techniques can also be used.

Inlay

This technique is used on flat, sugarpasted surfaces and is suitable where repeating patterns are required particularly if they have small elements needing accuracy. Sugarpaste the surface in the normal way and mark the pattern by pricking with a pin. Use a metal cutter to remove small areas of sugarpaste and reveal holes which are then filled with soft royal icing (coloured as required). Imaginative and exciting effects can be achieved creating colour and texture within the body of the sugarpaste coating.

Mosaic

The Ancient Roman technique of creating pictures using small tiles of ceramic material can be easily recreated in sugarwork. Flowerpaste is the ideal medium for this. Colour the flowerpaste as required and then roll out to an even thickness (using spacer bars) and cut out squares and leave to dry. The size of the squares will be relative to the size of picture you are making. When the tiles have hardened lay them in position on a bed of soft royal icing.

Pleating

This is a neat and tidy alternative to the garrett flounce. The sugar required is a blend of sugarpaste and flowerpaste to give strength when handling.

Pleating 1.

Roll the paste out on a non stick surface until quite thin. Cut as long a strip as possible to the required width using an icing ruler and sharp knife. Trim and neaten all edges. Mark even spacing (a small notch only) along the top edge, dependent upon the width of pleat required. Lift paste to join first two notches, lightly pinch together at top edge and lay over to one side to form pleat. Repeat as required. Trim and neaten paste and then glue to cake with gum arabic. Continue until the cake is complete.

Pleating 2.

Roll the paste out on a non stick surface until quite thin. Cut a strip of paste using a long, straight garrett frill cutter. Using a cocktail stick or similar, lift every alternate curved section and pinch at the top edge and then flatten to create a box pleat. Repeat this along the full length of paste and glue down the pleats with a touch of egg white at the top edge only. To create a lacy effect cut a pattern of small holes on the flat curved section using a small plain tube, i.e. No.1. Transfer on to the sugarpasted cake and secure with gum arabic. Continue in this way until the cake is complete.

Flower Modelling

The following rules apply to all the instructions for the making of the flowers in this book. To keep the individual instructions as brief as possible we have not repeated these rules for every flower.

SO DON'T FORGET THEM.

1. Knead the paste well before use to soften. Sticky paste is counteracted by adding more vegetable fat, stiff paste is counteracted by adding more egg white and white fat. Soft, stringy paste can be strengthened by microwaving on defrost and re-kneading. If this is not adequate, additional gum tragacanth may be added.
2. The use of white vegetable fat will allow you to roll your paste out much thinner than by using cornflour which tends to dry the paste out too quickly.
3. When making flowers with cutters, always soften the cut edge with a ball tool.
4. By pressing harder with the ball tool, the petals will gain movement and make them more realistic.
5. Cupping - rotate the ball tool in the centre of the cut petal shape.
6. Feeding wire into paste - paste must be thick enough to hold the wire, either by cutting thick paste and thinning edges, or by rolling paste to the two thicknesses before cutting.
7. Glueing - can be done with egg white or gum arabic
8. Patience - so often needed when petals need to be partially set before assembly.
9. Study - the real flower whenever possible as they always tell the true story. We believe there is no right or wrong way of making any item, provided the end result is what YOU want.
10. Assembly - always ensure that bare wires are covered with tape.
11. Steaming - petal dusted flowers and leaves tend to look 'dusty' and therefore unnatural. Steaming removes this dusty look and helps to 'set' the colour. Hold the flower or leaf in a fast jet of steam from a boiling kettle for a few seconds and leave to dry. Be careful not to make the petals too wet or they will become limp and collapse, or will fall off the wire. If you need to reshape a petal this method is useful.
12. NEVER EVER PUSH WIRES INTO AN EDIBLE PRODUCT (e.g. the cake) There are many suitable holders on the market, made of food grade plastics, that you can use. We ask that you never hide the holders by pushing deep into a cake or by covering with icing, etc. In fact, ensure that the recipient (or the person cutting the cake) knows that you have used a plastic holder.

Yellow Butterfly Flower

Using small template cut from yellow paste. Place a wire (28g) through the body of the butterfly, bend the wings backwards to give a closed effect and gently curl the tips of the wings. Place two yellow stamens in the head of the butterfly and allow to dry. Make four.
Dust - wings with yellow, body and wingtips with brown, orange spots on each wing. To complete, take four butterflies, holding together so that the stamens meet in the middle, creating the centre of the flower. Tape together.

White Butterfly Flower

Using small template cut from white paste. Place a wire (28g) through the body of the butterfly, bend the wings backwards to give a closed effect and gently curl the tips of the wings. Place two white stamens in the head of the butterfly and allow to dry. One only required for each flower.
Dust - body with pale green. To complete, bend the wire gently to an arch, hanging the butterfly flower upside down. Assemble two or three together on one stem.

Orchid Butterfly Flower

Using small template cut from white paste. Curl bottom wing upwards and inwards and place in orchid former. (This is the centre of the flower). Cut large template from white paste, put a wire (28g) down through the body and right angles to the wings, fold an angle in the wire and bed this down, 'glue' the smaller butterfly over the top, aligning the wings, and covering the flat section of wire. Make 3 petals and wire. When dry, tape in under the centre, one at the top, and one on each side, evenly spaced. Dust with pale peach and brown tones.

Water Lily

The waterlilies are constructed in polystyrene apple trays. Cut a calyx using a rose calyx cutter. This will not be seen but is needed to support the first layer of petals. Roll out white paste and light green paste, laying the white on top of the green and re-roll. Cut out 5 petals using template A. Ball each petal to curl and fix a petal to each sepal of the calyx. Cut 9 petals using template B from white paste only, ball each petal and fix these evenly on top of the first row, supporting each with a little tissue to lift. Repeat process with 9 petals using template C. Make stamens using yellow paste pushed through a sieve and glue these to the centre of the flower. When the flowers are dry, remove the tissue and lightly dust with pink colour.

Water Lily (miniature)

Cut template twice. Ball and cup. Glue one inside the other. Sprinkle yellow dust in the centre to give the impression of stamens.

Lilypad

Cut circles of green paste, using a round cutter. Cut out a wedge of paste. Lightly flute the edges with a ball tool. Mark with a veining tool and allow to dry. Dust with shades of green and brown colour. Glaze with confectioners varnish.

Lilypad (miniature)

Cut template and trim as shown in diagram, vein and ball slightly round edges.

Water plant leaf

Use the whole of the little heart shaped template, cut and vein and soften edge.

Honeysuckle

Take a small pea of paste and work to a cone shape on a dowel. Use a scalpel to cut one large and four small petals. Trim the large petal on both sides. Pinch and pull all petals, rounding the small ones and lengthening the larger one. Curve the single petal downwards, wire the flower on to 30g wire lengthening the neck of the flower, make a bunch of six stamens (one longer for the stigma), glue cut ends and push into throat of flower. Buds - a small ball of paste worked onto a 30 g wire, lengthening the neck. Make leaves. Tape all together.

Bulrush

Cover a 3"(7.5cm) length of 24g wire with a thin sausage of brown paste and leave to dry. Make the centre section of the bulrush by rolling a sausage shape in brown paste, 3" (7.5cm) long and glue on to a covered stub wire. Place the dried thin section into the top of centre section and leave to dry. Texture the centre section of the bulrush by moistening with gum arabic and rolling in semolina. Dust with brown colour. Leaves - roll out a long narrow strip of green paste and brush centre with gum arabic,lay a 28g wire onto it and fold the paste over.Trim away excess paste to give a long leaf about 1/4"(6cm) wide .Bend the leaf so that it curls at the top,lay down and leave to dry.Make several leaves at varying lengths. Dust with shades of yellow and brown colour.

Iris

Colour the paste as required and using 28g wire make a long slender bud about 2/3rds the length of template A, making sure the bud is very pointed. Roll out some paste and cut two petals using template A and slightly frill edges. Glue all but top 1/4 of petal and wrap round bud. Repeat on opposite side. With green paste, cut two of template A, cup slightly and mark the length of the centre with a veiner. Glue these as calyx leaving top 1/3rd of bud showing. For the partly opened flower, make the bud centre and cut three petals with template A, frill and cup slightly. Secure petals to bud overlapping each one. Cut 3 petals using template C leaving a thickened ridge down the centre. Frill top edge of each petal with a cocktail stick, turn over, cup well, turn back again and then turn up the frilled edge. Glue petals into position turning some petals down more than others. Make a calyx (see bud) and fix to flower having the tips of the calyx behind two of the petals.

The fully opened flower has individually wired petals. Cut 3 petals with template A. Frill the top half of each petal, curl the petal by running a ball tool down the centre, then mark a vein. Glue the bottom of the petal and fix to a wire, forming the petal into a tube with the join uppermost. Repeat with other 2. Cut 3 petals with template B. Cut through petal 1/3rd from top edge. Frill halfway down either side of the cut. Lightly cup the bottom of the petal and vein the centre. Glue a 28g wire through the centre vein almost to the cut, turn petal over and curl fluted end back, support with cotton wool until dry. Cut 3 petals with a thick centre, with template D. Lightly frill rounded end, dome the centre well with a ball tool and lengthen the pointed end with a ball tool, make a vein down the centre. Glue a 'V' at the pointed end of the petal and fix to the template B petals to make a type of mouth with the lips turned back. Leave to dry. Tape first three petals made, then add second set. Fix two green calyx pieces to the back of the flower. Dust as required.

Iris (Miniature)

Mould fine stems in green flowerpaste and leave to dry. Cut six petals and ball. Attach 3 petals pointing downwards and 3 petals pointing upwards. Buds are made by moulding a pea of paste (the size of the head of a glass headed pin) into a teardrop shape and wrapping one petal around. Attach to stem. Leaf - cut a sliver of green paste with a point at one end and vein with a cocktail stick. Leave to dry.

Pohutakawa

Wrap red cotton around two fingers 40 times, secure at the base with fuse wire, tape and cut off excess cotton. Mould a cone of green paste, hollow out the centre, apply glue and pull prepared centre through. To make buds, use a ball of red flowerpaste on a 28g wire. Take a ball of green icing, hollow the centre and cut 5 sepals evenly, working with a ball tool until they are long enough to almost cover the bud. Make the leaves with green flowerpaste and dust as required.

Petunia

Tape 5 stamens to a double 24g wire. Form a cone of paste, with a narrow back, and open up broad end with a cocktail stick or modelling tool, thinning the edge. Put the flower down over the template and cut where shown. Work the flower to give texture and vein the centre of each petal. Glue the wire with stamens in place and thin down the neck of the flower to make it slender. Dry. Calyx is formed from a cone of paste and hollowed out. Cut five 'V' shapes, thin down each sepal. Glue and slide into position behind flower.

Clematis (from "Honesty")

Wrap cotton around one finger, secure loops on to a wire and trim to half inch. Some flowers have four and some eight petals. Cut petals and wire individually with white wire. Ball tool and soften edges, make a ridge through the middle. Dust. Tape and make into arrangement.

Honesty

Make wire shapes for Honesty. Add a small piece of tape for the top. Roll paste thinly across the wire shape (which has been glued) trim, varnish, dust and wire into groups.

Snowdrop

Tape 3 small stamens to 28g wire. Cover with a small pea of white paste. Cut template A, cup each petal with ball tool and paint edge with green colour. Glue to stamens. Cut template B, again cupping into shape with ball tool. Glue to flower. Add a small pea of green paste to the back of flower. Make green foliage to complete by cutting thin strips of paste with a point at the top end. Glue to flower.

Aconite

Gather together a small bunch of medium stamens. Dust with green colour. Surround with approximately 15-20 small stamens and dust with yellow. Tape together on 26g wire. Make a former by shaping marzipan or sugarpaste into a ring, approx. 1" (2.5cm) diameter. Cover ring with tin foil and grease with white fat. Cut out green leaves using templates A and B, soften edges and lay into ring. (approximately 7 leaves). Glue together. Use template A cut 3 yellow petals, ball and place into position on ring. Glue. Cut 3 petals with template B, cup and glue to centre. Push stamens through centre and leave to dry.

Willow Catkin

Model a pea sized piece of flowerpaste onto a 33g wire and roll to a teardrop shape. Make a variety of sizes. Dip each one into glue and coconut that has been pulverised through a liquidiser, a micro size pea of brown paste is then glued to the base of each catkin. Tape in a natural arrangement on to florists stub wire and paint covered wire with coloured royal icing.

Alder Catkin

Mould sausage shaped pieces of flowerpaste on to 28g wire, dip in glue and then powdered gelatine. Once set dust with brown and skintone. Tape in a natural arrangement on to florists stub wire and paint covered wire with coloured royal icing.

Coelogyne Orchids

Make a column on 26g wire and leave to set. Cut template A, thin edges and vein as shown in diagram. Make small irregular cuts all along the large curve of the petal and lift with a cocktail stick to give shape. Wrap the throat around the column, glue and leave to dry. Cut two template B, soften, texture with corn husk and vein. Insert 28g wire and leave to dry curving backwards. Cut three template C, proceed as before but elongate one of these petals to at least 1.5 times longer than the others. Dry curved. Tape together.

Cattleya aurantiaca

This is a pulled flower. Cover a hook of 28g wire with a pea of paste and shape into a long column. Make a hole in the end with a pointed modelling tool and extend one edge to a point (this produces a long fine tube) This is the throat - set aside to dry. Make a teardrop shape of paste and place on to a dowel, make 5 even cuts, pinch and pull all petals, keeping a point at the tip. Thread wire through centre. Cut away any excess paste from the back of the flower if necessary.

Chrysanthemums

Cover a hooked 26g wire with a small pea of paste. Cut template D and cut petals in half and glue around pea of paste to make centre. Repeat three times. Cut template C three times, cut each petal in half and extend each petal widthways with a modelling tool or cocktail stick. Glue to flower and hang upside down to dry. Cut template B twice and repeat as above. Cut template B once, do not cut the petals in half but mark with modelling tool.

Glue to flower. Cut template A three times, mark one with modelling tool and glue to flower. Cut other two shapes completely in half, mark with modelling tool and glue to flower, leaving a small gap either side of the wire to increase the overall size of the flower. Use green paste and cut template E. Seal to underside of flower.

Alstroemeria

Tape together 6 small stamens, one longer than the others for the stigma, on 28g wire. Cut template A 3 times. Pinch a ridge into the centre back, thin, ball and insert 30g wire into the thicker ridge. Vein. Curve top back slightly. Pinch top edge together. When dry, colour and paint as required. Cut template B 3 times. Pinch a ridge into the centre back, thin edges, insert 30g wire, turn petal over and ball at top to make petal curve backwards. Texture with corn leaf and pinch a point at the top. When dry, dust petal tips with green. Tape the 3 'A' petals around stamens first and then tape the 'B' petals in the spaces left. Dust the outside of the petals with green at the base. Leaves - cut template A, elongate with ball tool, twist to give movement. Insert a 28g wire.

Lilac

Bud - attach a small ball of paste to a 30g wire and mark a cross at the top with scalpel. Open bud - as bud, then gently ease back each quarter section with a small ball tool. Flower - attach a small ball of paste to a 30g wire and flatten top with a modelling tool. Cut template, glue to flattened ball and prick a hole in the centre. Wire together in clusters, starting with buds and graduating to a larger shape with open buds and flowers and finishing on a 24g wire.

Japanese style Fantasy flower

Cut template 5 times leaving a thicker area at the wide end in which insert a 28g wire. Soften edges and elongate widthways and lengthways. Leave to dry. Make the centre by rolling a sausage shaped piece of paste on to a 28g wire, glue and roll in rice flour. Tape petals around centre.

Dendrobium Williamsonii

Cut template B five times from cream flowerpaste. Soften the edges, vein with corn husk and attach to 28g wire. Mould a column and leave to dry. To make the throat, cut template A twice from very thin paste. Moisten one with glue. Wind cotton around your finger approximately 20 times, cut in half, and place along front edge of glued throat. Place other one on top and seal together. Trim cotton with scissors. Soften and shape the throat, glue to column and leave to dry overnight. When dry, curl the the cotton threads by stroking with a metal edge, i.e. scissor blade. Dust inside of throat and around the outside at the base with orange. Dust petal edges green. Tape petals around central throat as shown.

Cattleya aurantiaca

This is a pulled flower. Cover a hook of 28g wire with a pea of paste and shape into a long column. Make a hole in the end with a pointed modelling tool and extend one edge to a point (this produces a long fine tube) This is the throat - set aside to dry. Make a teardrop shape of paste and place on to a dowel, make 5 even cuts, pinch and pull all petals, keeping a point at the tip. Thread wire through centre. Cut away any excess paste from the back of the flower if necessary.

Trichopilia tortilis

Make a small column. Cut one template A, frill the edges gently and attach to column. Petals - cut template B five times and insert a 28g wire in each. Soften edges and wind each round a cocktail stick and leave to dry. Dust throat with dark pink and paint on brown spots. Wire together.

Odontoglossum Rossii

Mould a very long column shape on to a 28g wire and leave to dry. Cut template B twice, soften, vein, insert a 28g wire and dry curving backwards. Cut one template C, elongate petals slightly, soften edge and vein. Make a small hole in centre and leave to dry curving forward. Throat - cut one template A and trim as shown. Soften, vein and frill edge. Glue to the base of the column but allow the column to stand proud of the throat when drying. Wire B petals to throat. Paint irregular blotches onto back petals (C) in reddish brown, thread onto wire behind throat and B petals and glue into position. Tape together.

Paphiopedilum insigne (slipper)

This is a pulled flower. Cover a hook of 28g wire with a pea of paste and shape into a small column. Take a larger pea of paste and cup centre to form a slipper. Thread wire through slipper and set aside to dry. Make a teardrop of paste and place on to dowel, make two cuts - one on either side. Make 3 more cuts evenly on one half, pinch and pull all petals, roll and soften edge, roll larger edge with cocktail stick. Thread column through centre of flower and leave to dry.

Magnolia

Make the centre first by rolling a sausage of green paste on to a 28g wire. Snip all over using pointed scissors. Leave to dry. Wind white cotton 50 times around finger, twist into a figure eight, wire and cut. Arrange around green pistil and dust. Trim cotton to 0.5" (1cm) Cut template A six times, Soften edge, texture with corn husk and mark central vein and dry curving inwards. Cut two template B, proceed as before but dry curving outwards. To assemble, tape 3 of template A petals around centre stamens, then add the other 3 petals overlapping the joins of the first three. Add the two B petals to opposite sides. Bud - glue a small sausage of paste, approximately 1" (2.5cm) long to a 26g wire. Cut template A twice. Soften, texture and vein each petal, wrap the first one around the centre and then the second one around the first. Shape the edges of the petals slightly.

Crocus

Make six stamens and one stigma by modelling tiny pieces of paste on to fine covered wire. Tape together and glue a tiny ball of paste to the base. Cut out two sets of petals and widen slightly using a ball tool, vein. Attach first set to stamens, wrapping gently and cupping as required. Attach second set of petals over the gaps between the first set. Paint the base of the flower rather than make a calyx.

Leaves - Cut thin slivers of green paste leaving a point at one end. Insert a wire at the other end and vein. When dry paint a white line down the centre and glaze.

Wisteria

You will need approximately 50 flowers, buds and pips for each spray. Shape the buds and pips as shown on 28g wire. Flowers - cut two template A, soften, overlap the two petals and glue to underside of a bud. Cut two template B, soften and vein, glue to the top of the bud, curving them upwards.

Pinks

Tape 2 white stamens to a 26g wire. Form a small mexican hat piece of paste and cut using template. Make tiny snips in the outer edge of each petal, thin and soften the petals, allowing the fringing to develop. Thread wire through and glue. Work a slender neck to the flower removing surplus paste if required. The calyx is slender and long. Form a small sausage pointed at one end, use cocktail stick to open this end and hollow out. Cut 5 'V' shapes and thin edges. Slide into position behind flower. Make further snips around base of calyx, two pairs opposite each other. Leaves - cut fine slivers of blue/green paste, pointed at one end and veined down the middle. Wire and leave to dry.

RECIPES

All recipes have been tested in metric weights. Conversion to imperial measurements have been carried out using 25g = 1oz

Rich Fruit Cake

250g	10oz butter
250g	10oz Silver Spoon Rich Dark Soft Sugar
250g	5 Eggs
5g	1tsp mixed spice
pinch	pinch salt
100g	4oz ground almonds
100g	4oz nougat paste (optional)
25g	1oz Silver Spoon Black Treacle
25g	1oz glycerin
300g	12oz plain flour
350g	14oz raisins
250g	10oz currants
350g	14oz sultanas
200g	8oz glace cherries (halved)
100g	4oz minced mixed peel (or finely chopped)
	zest and juice of one orange and one lemon

Prepare tins your favourite way. Preheat the oven 170°C (Gas 3), placing a small tin of water on the floor of the oven to create some humidity. Cream butter, sugar and nougat paste until light and fluffy. Add the eggs, in four stages, mixing well at each stage. Add flour, salt, spices and ground almonds and half mix into the mixture. Add all the cleaned fruit, the zest and juice of the orange and lemon, and the treacle and glycerin. Complete mixing. Weight the mixture according to the size of the tin (see chart) and bake for approximately 2 - 3.5 hours depending upon cake size. Remove from oven and whilst cakes are still hot pour in a mixture of one part glycerin and three parts dark rum. When cold, wrap in waxed paper, then tin foil, and leave to mature, preferably for one month.

Depth of cakes 3" (7.5cm). Approximate weights for:

	Square		Round	
5"	900g	2lb 4oz	700g	1lb 12oz
6"	1,300g	3lb 4oz	1,000 g	2lb 8oz
7"	1,700g	4lb 4oz	1,350g	3lb 4oz
8"	2.400g	6lb	1,800g	4lb 8oz
9"	3,000g	7lb 8oz	2,300g	5lb 12oz
10"	3,800g	9lb 8oz	3,000g	7lb 8oz
11"	4,900g	12lb	3,800g	9lb 8oz
12"	5,500g	13lb 12oz	4,350g	10lb 10oz

Light Fruit Cake

(an alternative to the heavy fruit cake and keeps well)

For an 8" round cake, prepare the cake tin, heat the oven to 180°C (Gas 4) placing a pan of water on the floor of the oven to give some humidity.

5g	1 level tsp baking powder
pinch	pinch salt
160g	6.5oz butter
150g	6oz Silver Spoon Light Golden Soft Sugar
200g	4 Eggs
225g	9oz plain flour
100g	4oz ground almonds
10g	2tsp glycerin
	zest and juice of one orange
	few drops of vanilla flavour
400g	1lb fruit including glace cherries, glace pineapple, sultanas, stem ginger and rum soaked dried apricots (all chopped to the size of the sultanas)

Cream butter and sugar until light and fluffy. Add the eggs in four stages, mixing in well at each stage. Add flour and dry ingredients, and half mix. Add the cleaned fruit, flavourings and glycerin and complete mixing. Bake for 1 -1.5 hours. Remove from the tins when cold. This cake does not need to mature before use.

Genoese

(firm, for sculpturing)

For a 7" x 10" baking tray, lined with paper. Expected depth 1" (2.5cm) when baked. Preheat oven 180°C (Gas 4)

100g	4oz cake margarine
140g	5.5oz McDougalls Supreme Sponge Flour
170g	6.5oz Silver Spoon Caster Sugar
pinch	pinch salt
100g	2 Eggs
100ml	4 fl.oz milk
15ml	3tsp glycerin
	few drops vanilla flavour

Crumble the margarine and dry ingredients together. In a separate bowl mix the liquid ingredients together and gradually add to the dry ingredients over one minute on slow speed on mixer. Scrape down the mix before proceeding to beat for one minute of medium speed. Bake for approxiamately 20 minutes.

Swiss Roll

Prepare a 10" x 14" swiss roll tin with greaseproof paper. Preheat the oven to 230°C (Gas 8)

150g	6oz eggs
100g	4oz Silver Spoon Caster Sugar (warmed in oven)
90g	3.5oz plain flour (sieved twice)
10g	0.5oz ground almonds

Whisk the warm sugar and eggs together in very clean, greasefree bowl, until you achieve a very firm foam. Gently fold in the flour and almonds, taking great care to keep as much air in the mixture as possible, i.e. do not overmix. Bake for about 5 minutes in a hot oven. When cool, fill and roll carefully.

Continental Buttercream

180ml	7fl. oz water
620 g	1lb 9oz Silver Spoon Granulated Sugar
250g	5 Eggs
675g	1lb 11oz butter

Boil sugar and water together until 118°C (softball). Whisk the eggs until you achieve a firm foam and whilst still whisking, pour on the hot sugar solution. Continue to beat on a high speed until cool. Add soft butter in small knobs whilst beating. Flavour and colour as desired.

Royal Icing

60g	3oz pure hen albumen
480ml	1 pint water
3kg	7lb Silver Spoon Icing Sugar

Whisk the albumen into the water using greasefree equipment. Leave to soak for at least one hour and preferably overnight, in the refrigerator. Sieve into the machine mixing bowl and gradually add the icing sugar on slow speed. Keep covered to prevent crusting.

Pastillage

400g	10oz royal icing
200g	8oz Silver Spoon Icing Sugar
10g	2 tsp Gum Tragacanth

Sieve the icing sugar and the gum and knead into the royal icing. Keep in a plastic bag.

Modelling Marzipan

1Kg	2lb 2oz Raw marzipan
125g	5oz liquid glucose
750g	1lb 14oz Silver Spoon Icing Sugar

Warm the glucose and mix into the raw marzipan. Add the icing sugar in three stages and knead well. Keep in a plastic bag.

N.B. If the mixture begins to oil add Orange Flower Water or Rose Water. Gentle handling will prevent oiling. Do not use the marzipan at extreme temperatures, (too hot/too cold)

Rock Sugar

500g	1lb 4oz Silver Spoon Granulated sugar
120ml	5fl.oz water
60g	2.5oz liquid glucose
50g	2oz royal icing (colour as desired)

Boil the sugar and water together until 118°C (softball). Add glucose (do not stir). Continue boiling to 132°C (soft crack). Remove from the heat, plunge the pan into cold water to prevent further cooking. Using a wooden spoon mix in the royal icing. At this stage your mixture erupts. Quickly pour into a large glass bowl in which has been placed a sheet of greaseproof paper. Allow to cool, break up and use as required.

Glue

We recommend different 'glues' for different jobs or mediums.

Pastillage	Royal icing with a pinch of gum tragacanth added for strength
Flowerpaste	1. Egg white (fresh or pure albumen solution) 2. Gum arabic (1 part) and rose water (3 parts) warmed to ease incorporation 3. Flowerpaste mixed with egg white
Marzipan	If necessary - glue with chocolate or gum arabic, never royal icing